Toulouse

Horst Keller

# Lautrec: Painter of Paris

Harry N. Abrams, Inc. *Publishers* New York

Translated from German by Erika Bizzarri

Frontispiece: photograph of Henri de Toulouse-Lautrec at the age of thirty

Title page: *Invitation to a Glass of Milk* (detail). 1900. Lithograph

Library of Congress Catalog Card Number: 69-12478
Copyright 1968 in Germany by Verlag M. DuMont Schauberg, Cologne
All rights reserved. No part of the contents of this book may be
reproduced without the written permission of the publishers
Harry N. Abrams, Incorporated, New York

Printed and bound in West Germany

# Contents

Henri de Toulouse-Lautrec . . . . . . . . . . . 7

Chronology . . . . . . . . . . . . . . . 82

List of Colorplates . . . . . . . . . . . . . 107

List of Black-and-White Plates . . . . . . . . 108

List of Text Illustrations . . . . . . . . . . . 109

# Henri de Toulouse-Lautrec

The art of Henri de Toulouse-Lautrec is still modern, despite the fact that his modest life span of thirty-seven years ended at the threshold of the twentieth century. The explanation of this modernism is simple: it lies in Lautrec's compelling passion for representing man and life. Man is the center around which all thinking and creating revolve, and all periods, including our own, have been oriented to man. Lautrec's leitmotiv is the exploration and experiencing of humanity, whom he endowed with "eternal" presence, and it is this part of the artist that has been transmitted with undimmed intensity.

Toulouse-Lautrec's art remains ever fresh. It has always commanded attention and cultivates our awareness of the underlying essentials. Julius Meier-Graefe called Lautrec, the creator of many paintings and drawings, of radiant posters and lithographs, the "Essence of Paris."

Neither his era, his living habits, nor the tragedy of his dwarfism or the course of his life and its decline has retained great importance or meaning. The anecdotes about Lautrec do not explain his art; they serve only as guideposts. On the one hand they are intended to amuse, and on the other to arouse sympathy. They reveal a range of superficial involvement from delight, to ecstasy, to aversion, to outright revulsion for the *fin-de-siècle* world and the way of life of Montmartre. After almost seven decades

the repertory of stories about the crippled Viscount Henri de Toulouse-Lautrec Monfa has been exhausted. All the sympathetic, witty, illustrative, and colorfully characterized representations which appeared in the decades after 1926 culminated on the centenary of his birth in the publication of a "dossier" of his life and art (*Lautrec by Lautrec*, New York, 1964). All that remains is for medical science to explain the interrelationship between his deformity and his art.

But isn't the continuing involvement with the genius of Lautrec a sure sign that his "presence" is as valid today as yesterday, that his innate skill and mastery of the medium surmount any doubts as to whether he shared in that basic fund of humanity, free from cynicism, which is indispensable for the creation of a truly human art capable of intensifying and preserving life?

He expected of his models only that they let him paint them as he saw them. Yvette Guilbert objected only a little to being portrayed so sharply by Lautrec. She finally autographed the volume of lithographs dedicated to her—unique in their intimate association with a single theatrical personality.

This indicates both Lautrec's caustic attitude toward the scintillating participants in the life of Montmartre and the sympathy which he proffered to those fettered to such a milieu during their remarkable, yet quickly fading careers: the wag and the buffoon, the singers and the cabaret dancers, and the women of the brothels.

Intermittent pauses gave him not so much the opportunity for relaxation as for experimentation with increasingly forceful brushwork and more audacious descriptions of an uncompromising world of motifs, which the superiority of his artistic perception permitted to survive the days of crass actuality and short-lived fame. From our point of view Lautrec's intention was not so much to fix the image of an epoch as it was to endow a moment with duration, as Ingres intended in his *Odalisque* and Manet in his *Olympia*.

A picture of the period is offered by Lautrec's contemporaries who posed with him for photographs and became his indispensable foil; being the smallest member of the group, he was always conspicuous. In each group that passes in review in the venerable brown-tinged documentary photographs—the entire atelier of Cormon, the group of painters of the *Revue Blanche*, friends, or models—Lautrec projects a casual aloofness even when grotesquely dressed or playing the buffoon. One would be tempted to relate his aloofness to his noble upbringing and birth were not his ability to see himself as an impersonal observer so evident. This ability enabled him to examine with an unerring eye the Parisian pleasure district of Montmartre, which he chose as his adopted home.

At this time Montmartre was being transformed from a place of semirural, semi-improvised popular entertainment to a quarter of organized diversion. He subjugated it to his ideas and only then did it become art. Tirelessly working, drawing, sketching, observing the same places at the same hours—at a ball, at a café concert, at the circus, and at many other places—he constantly studied until he knew by rote a certain movement, a gesture, a figure transforming itself into an ornament. He saw these details more clearly than anyone else, and it is this which constitutes the enduring magic of his "dance of figures," images of which emerge in the studies and paintings in

the museum of his native Albi and in the galleries of the New World and the Old. The frivolity of his environment and its heroes is accurately mirrored there while being elevated to a sphere of timelessness. As our insight grows, we are astounded to discover that, contrary to expectation, the involvement of Lautrec's art with its period in no way diminishes its relevance for us today.

Just what is it that makes Lautrec's works so captivating? Iridescent, rich in imaginative forms, interspersed with wit and rare insights, inspired by the fascination of a single moment, his is an art full of a passionate self-assertion expressed in a unique choice of colors and motifs. The immediacy of Lautrec's art can be attributed to a careful focusing and a thoroughly understood and deeply felt drawing, which provides every living thing with an inner framework.

Only a few significant paintings, sketches, lithographs, and posters appear in this volume as representative of his collected works—perhaps as many as could once have been hung in a little art store on the Rue Laffitte during the lifetime of a rather small *grand seigneur* in frock coat and derby, with a cane and pince-nez, Toulouse-Lautrec himself.

There was never a day in his life that he actually had to paint. If he had wanted he could have done nothing but observe to his heart's content the world into which he had chanced to be born, to be entertained by it, to use it for his own diversion, to see it in the light of a long-vanished noblesse. And yet he painted almost every day up to his early death: no landscapes, no still lifes, rarely inanimate objects, only bare indications of space, but human beings, men and women, particularly girls, nearly all of whom he depicted in the full expression of their being, the women displaying their feminine allures, dancing, singing, glancing, noisy—or even more impressive in their silence.

His is an adult world of emotions ranging from the heights to the depths. The dramaticism is restrained only

by the greater drama of Lautrec's line and color, as in the chansons of Yvette Guilbert; the explosive dancing feet of Valentin and La Goulue; the thundering voice of the loutish Aristide Bruant; Jane Avril, delicate and exalted, a tender creature of the dance, neither beautiful nor ugly, but an exclamation of being; Yvette Guilbert taking her curtain call, fully savoring her success as queen of Montmartre; and many others, aligned in procession, once the lifeblood of their world, attuned more to decadence than to success—now all mute, motionless, forgotten, except as a picture by Lautrec.

What led up to his paintings and how did his pictures come to be?

In 1881, Lautrec was in Paris. Always a sickly child, two early accidents crippled his legs so that, although he was only seventeen, his long experience of suffering had already matured him. Paris accepted and helped him to go on as she had so many others, not destructively, but challenging him to fulfill his destiny (a gift more awesome than his high birth) to become the painter of Montmartre.

This deformed son of one of the oldest families of French nobility, with a rural tradition of southern French feudalism which was even then somewhat anachronistic, found himself on a new, undreamed-of stage of life. Initially relying only upon his still-developing talent, he was not yet hardened to his existence. The Parisian world of artists and of the demimonde hastened the ruin of many others who found themselves in an analogous situation—without achievement, without inspiration, without ideas, drowning their pain by satiating their appetites.

Lautrec soon reacted to the state of abandon and personal anguish in which he found himself and which cannot well be described. All accounts of his life, even contemporary ones, underscore the spiritual acumen and sound brain with which he soon seized hold of this life. He was shortly to reveal himself as a most incredible mixture of extremes, possessing as he did an uncontain-

able joy of life in a stunted, dwarflike body, an aristocratic indifference together with a genuine frenzy for painting, and the naïve warmheartedness of a denizen of Montmartre combined with a cool aloofness. The enthusiasm of the novice was restrained by the strength of his character. And all this in order to scrutinize a whole world of new faces as no one else had done or was to do, except perhaps the young Picasso, who lost his Spanish melancholy with Lautrec and followed him a few significant steps farther on this path.

His congenial contemporaries—Vuillard, Bonnard, and the quieter talents such as Maurice Denis, Paul Ranson, Sérusier, and Félix Vallotton, who were at the moment being featured in the Natanson brothers' periodical *La Revue Blanche*, and even their great master and predecessor Degas—remained at the threshold of this

dubious world, which could be entered only with the utmost open-mindedness. They clung to their art, to their marvelous colors and their multitude of masterly strokes. As long as they were left in peace to paint, they contented themselves with a homely omelette for lunch, perhaps shared by a visitor. But otherwise their work regime, the discipline of their creating, their concentration on seeing and painterly transformation was their one and only law. Their creations escaped the importunities of the all too obvious and the quickly definable.

With Lautrec it was different. He willingly risked being considered a facile person and a facile artist, or at least seeming to be one. What he sought was a proximity to the outcast, and even more, to the willfully outcast, to the reality of life and vice, to mockery and cynicism, to any number of poisons, even to the most harmful kinds of costly alcoholic beverages. And when this talented young artist who painted animals in the style of Géricault—still protected and limited by conventions of thinking and painting—had found all this, fifteen years were left in which he could paint people. These years describe a great arc. Lautrec had the courage to descend into the depths of iniquity and to seek that which is human precisely there. Prior to him only Félicien Rops, with obvious relish, and once Degas, Raffaelli, and Constantin Guys ventured to approach the subject, each in his own way, undaunted and sometimes even demonic.

His friends, the clients of the café concerts, cabarets, and dance halls, the performing singers, the male and female clowns, form the variety of figures who appeared first in the leaves of his sketchbook, then in his painted cardboards, and then in his canvases. It was not long before they also became subject matter for his lithographs. Before venturing to give form to a world which no one till then had elevated to the dignity of art, Lautrec had to learn lithography from scratch under Chéret and especially Père Cotelle. Only then was he ready to transform with consummate decorative unity what he saw

into a pictorial reality of three- or four-color prints with intuitively chosen colors, or of black-and-white lithographs with translucent tones, often caught by an encompassing powerful line, a stroke of genius, so that these posters and lithographs stand on equal footing with the paintings.

Through a significant use of such artistic means Lautrec handed down to posterity the inexorably rushing earthly days of all these carefree figures. Their actual physical appearance, often quite insignificant, was relatively unimportant to him. What really mattered was a touch of *esprit*, their impulsiveness, their brilliant wickedness, the fascinating fashionable attire (probably quite modest in reality), as well as their laughter, their smiles, their grimaces, their complaints, their pantomimed stage whispers, the whole merry, fully orchestrated rise and fall of life. He dedicated a separate chapter to the wonderful and eccentric movements of his extravagant models, particularly the dancers.

Ever since Lautrec's friend Maurice Joyant gave a close-up portrait of the artist, others have chimed in again and again to praise the uniqueness of his art, some in strong defense, others in quiet wonder. Generally their first obstacle was the environment in which he worked. When the life of the brothels was involved their language became circumlocutory; words were inadequate to describe the despairing love affairs of the girls among themselves; and the realism of a brothel, seen from close up, became oppressive. It was a mistake to decorate Maupassant's *La Maison Tellier* with Lautrec's lithographic series *Elles*, for the joyous, burlesquing material of the former distorts the art form of these incomparable color lithographs.

Lautrec's art is to be judged by how he represented the overpowdered *diseuses* and dancers on stage at the cabaret, in the *chambres séparées*, on the dance floor, and in the bars. It cannot easily be compared with the art of some of his contemporaries who overcharged their subject matter so as to leave the observer speechless.

Suppose we were to forget both the subject matter and the fact that art can ennoble the ignoble, transform a junkman's cart into a gala coach, and turn sleazy dancers' costumes into shimmering robes. It would mean trying to feel one's way into the heart of these paintings and to see them for their own sakes. They deserve such an attitude, for Lautrec's paintings have never been as well known as his lithographs and posters. The rapid diffusion of the latter brought him fame during his lifetime, whereas his paintings continued to be officially banned from exhibitions and even from the Luxembourg Museum in Paris.

By looking at these pictures without prejudice or embarrassment the door is opened to a completely frank dialogue. This proposal for a fresh approach to Lautrec's work, in the manner suggested, is possible only because the work of describing his life and art has already been done. Beginning with Joyant, Lautrec's friend and the custodian of his surviving works, many have tried to illuminate the varied facets of the painter's life—the strangest of the moderns, including Van Gogh—through his intimacy with the life around him. When one is aware, for example, that traffic regulations were nonexistent in the Paris of 1890 and that charabancs and coaches had to drive skillfully around groups of pedestrians chatting in the middle of the boulevard, the fact is assimilated with one's concept of the painter and his models.

The point of departure which takes a knowledge of Lautrec's life history for granted or which limits itself to providing a *pro memoria* addenda of a few dates leads one to discuss the pictures themselves, the sketches, their execution, and the compositions based on them. The opportunity then arises to describe the various methods the painter used to reach his goal, which he did in the least time and by the shortest route.

Lautrec was a persevering worker, even though he seemed to work effortlessly. The compelling force was not magic, but most probably mania. In fact our purpose in the following pages is to point out just that.

We shall therefore bypass Lautrec's youth, in which he tested his talent for drawing while patiently lying abed, as well as his short-lived studies with the deaf-mute animal painter Princeteau, chosen by his father. The influence of Cormon, whose atelier he attended and who offered him friendship as well as advice, was also relatively unimportant. Not till their paths separated and Lautrec rented a studio in Rue Caulaincourt did his painting begin to acquire characteristic features of its own. The decently dressed, rather stub-nosed "almost ladies," who however knew how to hold a parasol and to keep a pose, whom he painted in the garden of Père Forest, were just the right models for the peculiar motion of Lautrec's brush, precipitous at one moment and dragging the next. He painted in oil, only barely covering the cardboard or canvas, achieving an effect closer to tempera but which could also have been achieved with crayons.

Interwoven like the countless colored, exactly tuned wires of a relay station, the brush strokes move over the rounded bosoms of the models, over the short sleeves, and form their hair with wires of color. This is the style of a restrained fury, for which slowness meant "love," and persistence was for the sake of accuracy in the joy of painting a human being and of painting him credibly.

The brush strokes which Lautrec invented here were to remain his own unique achievement. Some contemporaries and critics accused him of taking no pains with space, of not changing his methods in order to develop his picture in depth. But he sought just the opposite, a characteristic determined only in part by a study of Japanese color wood-block prints and of color lithographs. The limitation of space to a mere indication runs throughout his work. It is also a sign of the limited duration of each specific involvement and of his capacity to work on a picture only so long as it fully occupied his attention, only as long as was essential. "Focus" meant brevity.

He used the surface of the brown or brownish card-

board, glued in layers and probably prepared or fixed (for the years have hardly altered its tone) as part of the picture itself: a garden wall, the inside of a studio, the hazy interior of a bar, or part of a street scene. The undefinable dry-earth color is just barely noticeable as a pervasive lightness in the picture itself, emerging through branches, foliage, carpets, clothing, hair, and skin as a flecked ocher-colored ground. It serves only as a sober counterpart to the colored patches of chalk which seem to strive to obliterate this tenacious ocher ground. As is the case with tempera, the applied color is often powdery and pale, and only individual passages are finished.

A question presents itself at this point: Is there any other material on which, in this *Belle Époque* as it was often called, Lautrec's dance of figures from a "borrowed Olympus" could possibly have been fixed in such a convincingly beautiful way? An indication, which the fully executed canvases fail to obscure, is provided by the sketches in the Toulouse-Lautrec Museum of Albi.

Lautrec apparently chose this cardboard, which his contemporaries, particularly Vuillard, often preferred to canvas, because it lent itself to an intellectual treatment. While it may also have impeded the spatial development, it was ideal for keeping all statements about space as fluctuating as possible, whether in the case of Lautrec or of someone else. Another factor was his sudden flare of enthusiasm for a model, a pose, a scene, a focal point of bearing or gesture, or for the physical peculiarity of the material. As soon as the subject had been nailed fast in a striking and caustic characterization, whether on paper, canvas, or cardboard, his enthusiasm quickly waned. As if in conscious reference to photographic seeing, or perhaps because the scenes depicted were never imaginary but always actually seen, the figures were often placed close to one edge or with a portion of a garment left out of the picture.

This might occasionally result in apparent improvisations and not form a coherent composition, yet the impression remains that a fleeting, irretrievable moment in the human comedy of errors has been saved from hopeless oblivion through the art of Lautrec.

A renunciation of space is however quite coherent with the way of seeing peculiar to Lautrec, particularly striking upon observation of his pictures and sketches. It can only partially be explained by a fascination with the then new possibilities of photography, although we do find examples of foreshortening that could have been learned only from photography: a pushing together of space and a drawn-out perspective alien to painting, in dancing couples, in race horses, and in the famous circus rider (now in Chicago), in which the heavy Belgian horse seems to be lost in the space of the arena.

But Lautrec's mode of seeing was unique in its artistic awareness of the climax of the moment of encounter between the artist and his human subject, the moment when brush is touched to canvas to portray the human body, the appearance of a particular face, the outline of a profile, the delineation of a back, the language of hands and feet, the interlacing and positioning of limbs (often still in photographic foreshortening), as well as the expressions of apathy and tension and forced gaiety, which are a part of the sphere of metropolitan entertainment. All the models involved in his pictures, even the dandified gentlemen in top hats, play their various roles in this atmosphere of surging and waning entertainment. Whatever their individual peculiarity, Lautrec saw them as part of a whole. Patiently they posed for him, even flattered by the fact, without the inner aversion which was felt by those who posed for a portrait by the newcomer from Leghorn, Modigliani.

Lautrec, with an all-encompassing frenzy for participation, included even the drowsing marginal figures of populated scenes. They are often the only indication as to where the principal actors are to be found. Most striking of all is the fact that this small, sharp-eyed painter frequently looked down on his models—his is definitely not what one might call an ant's-eye view. Lautrec sketching must be visualized somewhere up behind the dancers, clowns, and the reclining and seated persons looking over their shoulders, or in the top tier at the circus, or standing on a table at a bar, or perching on the railing of the Moulin de la Galette or on the brass knob of a bedpost like Tom Thumb. From his vantage point he gazed on faces, coiffures, hats with cascades of feathers, fur tippets, garments, gauze, on a feather boa, on skin, or on a colorful, lifelike interior scene of a boudoir. The spiritual and visual overcompensation of this dwarflike being for a visual angle which nature had denied him is astounding. In this way he lets one forget his physical condition. Only then do his words take on meaning: "I have never been anything more than a crayon, all my life!"

This approach also permitted him to delve into the scene whenever he wished. The standpoint of his focus, from which he tried to pinpoint his subjects, lay above or below the stage of life. His penetrating scrutiny of this world of figures in full action permitted only a short pause before the scene flitted by and the moment of inspiration vanished, unless Lautrec patiently awaited its return or reconsidered and reworked what he had seen in his studio. He exercised an unimaginable concentration in every artistic purpose and came succinctly to the point in his execution, whether from below or from above. It was this gift which gave him his innate superiority; he remained the master of each and every scene.

To recapitulate: Lautrec, the confident expert of the Montmartre milieu which ungrudgingly accepted him, and which had its hard and fast rules just as in the world outside, emancipated himself from identification with pleasure seekers and pleasure. He was an eye, curiously mute and scrutinizing, seeking no intimacy. The persons portrayed in turn look out of his pictures at us, often with the gravity of an animal or with the uninhibited air of a person who believes himself alone.

New facets of Lautrec's character are revealed by the fact that he was also capable of drawing and painting the more intimate details as well as the over-all scene, with the efflorescence of faces in the stage lights and the tension at the lining up of the quadrille at the Moulin Rouge. He had to feel himself a part of the group. His lack of disdain and his refusal to be pitied immediately swept aside the primary hindrance which might have been an obstacle to his acceptance. He was permitted to recount, figure by figure, the everyday life of this extraordinary world entirely in unvarnished and forthright images as none of his contemporaries succeeded in doing, rising above the simple role of picture reporter.

A selection of individual themes and thematic groups shows Lautrec in his capacity as the transforming eye of an environment. While on the whole his painting was not concerned with space, in those cases where surroundings were necessary for the intelligibility of the image, something similar to an indication of depth appeared. Such spatial construction might require an ordinary, unimpressive room casually furnished with wicker furniture, light tables, and dishes, or it might call for a collection of sofas as in a *salon*. But never, even for a moment, was the main *human* subject lost sight of. Nor does anything resembling still life evolve in these pictures. The sketchy spatial indications carefully calculated as complements to the person represented unfold in the distant background in the form of a brilliant sham architecture, exotic, pseudo-Baroque, Orientally overladen, never taken seriously, but in every case a persuasive sorcery, ranging from a modest to a really elegant, even luxurious, composition. Often it was just the wall mirrors which multiplied the room, reflected the whirling ball of figures or a single figure from all sides, confounding front and back, as Manet had done in the *Bar at the Folies-Bergère*.

Lautrec's artistic point of view was always consonant with the attitude of a *grand seigneur*, an attitude that seems to have been automatically determined. The narrative character of many pictures is only a superficial

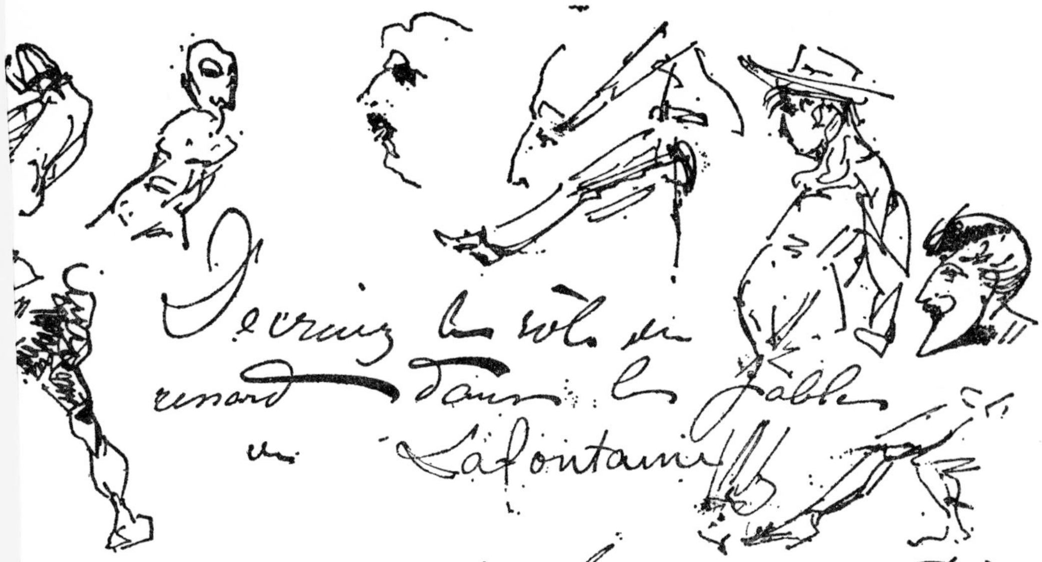

Décrire le rôle du
renard dans les fables
de Lafontaine

[...]animaux ont fourni un contingent
considérable à l'apologue que le
renard. Esope débuta en le mettant
en scène. Phèdre suivit pour lui de
motifs raffinés. Le moyen âge lui
même se sert des ~~personnes~~, directeurs / chroniqueurs pour
écrire le roman du Renard. Lafontaine
recueillit avec amour cet héritage de
ses devanciers.
Plus que ~~tout~~ autre il donna au caractère
changeant de Compère le Renard
ces ~~tours~~ si ingénieux. Le trait principal
en est la tromperie: tromper les
autres! Quel beau résultat. Quelle finesse
met il en usage, la ruse, lorsqu'il
invente le coup à venir goûter le bon
fromage qui n'est autre que la lune.
Le loup descend et le contrepoids amène
le meunier. Puis le voilà courtisan couronné

patina. The observer can ascertain that the fleeting exterior reality soon gave way to an unchanging optical reality. It seems that the nature of Lautrec's artistic temperament completely excluded "finger exercises," yet he never tired of painting and painting still more. He approached the scene to be represented in a state of mental stimulation and always placed what the eye saw above that which the brain could devise. Yet in every case he offered more than what he was given. Both for him and for the modern observer, this means that, in his painting as well as his drawing, he was unfailingly capable of exteriorizing the underlying spiritual qualities and that he unceasingly drew upon this resource. His exultation over an unexpectedly grand and particularly suitable subject or in the coincidence of a concept and the available setting, search as we may throughout this volume, did not result in a single false step in his choice of means. There are no awkward additions, nothing has been painted over or covered that might dissolve the enchantment. When the medium was oil rather than tempera, he handled his brush appropriately, using shorter strokes and covering his ground in a manner different from his usual way of working. He even went to the extreme of using stippled highlights in the outermost areas of light as in classical oil painting, and the delicacy of color relates him to the French tradition, where he is otherwise difficult to place, for there too Lautrec was an outsider. But if all of Lautrec's artistic resolutions are critically examined, it becomes clear that he was in harmony with his means of expression. (In this respect the obvious thoughtlessness of his forgers eventually gives them away.)

Lautrec never seems to have been in doubt as to how a subject was to be descriptively or satirically resolved. Even as a very young artist he must have had an amazing knowledge of living things, of the external as well as internal structure of man and animal. The same infallible accuracy with which the adolescent Lautrec depicted the motion of horses (page 28) in the pages of his sketchbooks

and in small canvases was later to characterize his drawings of man and beast in action. A dancer enters the limelight; a hand comes to rest on the table; a face turns toward the observer; animated, living creatures are set in audacious overlappings into the rectangle of the picture. Always accurately and soundly observed, his subjects are convincing even in what remains hidden, even where color lithography has, as it were, canceled the sense of space, and our supposition of this space must necessarily coincide with Lautrec's abbreviations and with his sense for a decorative whole. He is the first artist who taught the public a new way of seeing, which he in turn had learned from the Japanese color prints.

This is most evident in his poster of Jane Avril dancing on stage at the Jardin de Paris (page 21), a print of worldwide fame. In the foreground the neck of the bass viol, together with the hand and forearm, as well as the face of the musician, coalesce into an abstract ornament which encompasses the sheet of music, stage, and the brightly colored dancer, immersed in orange, yellow, and white who is the focal point. This is done with a softly slurring stroke which anticipates Art Nouveau and summarizes animate and inanimate into a wonderful abstraction.

Lautrec's work reveals no tormented questioning of the validity of his talent. It was as if he had known from the first day of his emergence as an artist that his time was measured. While his skill and restless activity were a way of blunting the poignancy of his voluntary exile from the sun and sheltering wealth of his home in southern France, his driving urge for creation, even his sense of mockery and wit, provided the necessary counterforces for his life. He overcame the obstacle of his extraordinary appearance in just this way, anticipating the laughter of others with such resoluteness that among the extant photographs of modern artists his are the most impressive, like the caricatures he drew of himself. Where he was not known, where he had to fear that he would not be accepted as a human being, he avoided

Miss May Belfort in der ›Irish and American Bar‹  ·  Miss May Belfort at the 'Irish and American Bar'

derision by adopting clothing that would lend him an aspect of authority. (Once in the summer when he went to the seashore, he donned the uniform of a merchant-marine captain.)

An often-redeeming dash of cynicism, an ever-acute spirit, a compulsive loquacity, a gift for pantomime, a sense of aloofness, his carefully chosen dress and his various gestures, including the giving of gifts, soon enough made him the master of his models regardless of the dubious proximity he may have had to them. Not everyone in Montmartre recognized the young painter immediately, and a dwarf serves for amusement, as he learned from a few thoughtless individuals and drifting skid-row characters. Lautrec dared to approach even creatures such as these who had waived their claim to human dignity. The bleakness of their feelings is reflected in the faces which he portrayed, faithfully recorded in response to his love of truth.

Even in the environment of the brothels, the freedom he enjoyed was more that of a master than a fool—here where coarse sensual enjoyment and slandering remarks could have suffocated the projects of a painter. His natural air of superiority together with a friendly approach enabled the models to pose for him with an intimacy which the visual image externalized. And thus a core of inviolable humanity appeared under the layers of trumpery and ill repute. But at this point Lautrec's mockery had long since ceased.

But now we shall turn to the individual pictures and themes, the main objective of this essay. The works discussed here range from 1888 to shortly before Lautrec's death in 1901. The first examples are therefore those of a young man of twenty-four who has found his own personal style.

This undertaking, to follow up individual pictorial inventions, is stimulated by the continuous spiritual enjoyment which the pursuit of his works elicits. Anyone who approaches a picture by Lautrec, in whatever part of the world, becomes absorbed with and is directly touched by his language of art. This fact by itself reveals still more about Lautrec. Temporal references and non-artistic components of his life story remain subordinate to such a consideration of his work. Dates and circumstances are known, his incentives communicated. In many famous texts the cleverness of the author goes hand in hand with the accomplishments of Lautrec himself, further testimony as to how much this painter has kindled the poetic tendencies of writers.

If we meet neither landscapes nor still lifes in our excursion into Lautrec's world of pictorial subjects, it simply means that he was not interested in reproducing nature or in illuminating inanimate things. In fact in his paintings he shunned Nature, which had cast him out, and only when he was in need of a vacation in the modern sense did Lautrec turn away from the city. His trips to the seaside, to England, and along the coast of France were moments of relaxation. The summer days he spent on a sailboat off the Normandy coast, preferably with his friend Joyant, were especially refreshing pauses.

Light as a phenomenon dominates his painting, being much more than just the gradual lightening of his palette. In some way or other all of his color sketches beginning with his *Portrait of Vincent van Gogh* (page 9) reveal this involvement. Painted as it is on cardboard in pastels, a technique seldom used by Lautrec, this portrait is perhaps the most luminous of all and is an early indication of Lautrec's talent. Austere, Van Gogh leans forward to converse with someone sitting across from him at the café table. A picture of concentration from his forehead to his interlaced hands resting upon the tablecloth, this great artist was Lautrec's radical opposite. Fanatic and persuasive, he arrived in Paris in 1886 from a harsh and frugal north and moved on to Arles two years later.

In swirling, sweeping parallel pastel strokes, only rarely crossed by opposing lines, the half-figure portrait moves toward the right. This type of pictorial composition, precisely either in profile or full-face, was charac-

teristic of Lautrec for a long time. A series of profile portraits seem to suggest that he wanted in this way to approach his models as closely as possible in order to study them with an almost scientific precision. Elusiveness and indefinability are qualities extraneous to his way of seeing. Even oblique views were razor sharp in their execution, for it was a matter of expressing personality through a basic precision of observation. In the portrait of Van Gogh, the extraordinarily sure outline of the sharp-cut features stands out against the much more richly illuminated area behind. The uniform lightness of the skin and reddish beard of the subject require so little internal drawing that the idea of a "reversed silhouette" can be broached. A certain singularity of the head against this background is heightened by the lively pictorial execution—close to the style of Van Gogh himself—all around the figure. With the aid of external factors, this portrait also documents a short friendship, elicited by an interchange of ideas in Cormon's atelier, which ended with Lautrec's suggestion that Van Gogh go to Arles, in other words to the same south where Lautrec himself had his roots. But actually the picture tells us of the singular fascination Lautrec felt for this diametrically opposed personality who chanced to arrive in Paris like a bird of passage and who was soon impelled to continue his voyage.

Van Gogh's first style of juxtaposed shaded strokes lingered on for a while in the work of Lautrec, who was eleven years his junior. The stroke and colors were thus chosen until he found his own harmony of line, that is until the time came when Lautrec was ready to abandon it for a sweeping line and finally arrived at his own inimitable style. On the whole his painting remained colored drawing until the end. One reason is that as soon as he had mastered a subject, he lost interest in it. Changing friendships and varied interests ensured that his range of figures represented a cross section of the life around him. This singular skill of abbreviating in a way all his own also explains why some of his lithographs are on a par with the finished paintings or the intermediate sketches.

The draftsmanlike sketch, which first characterized his style and therefore preceded the posters, and in particular his calligraphic interpretation, run parallel with his exposure to East Asian influences via the general popularity of the Japanese color wood-block print in France. These features are recognizable in a great number of prints and drawings of the end of the century in which the subject matter recalls the social criticism of Steinlen's drawings and those of other contemporary artists, and in some aspects was related to Daumier.

But the charcoal drawing of *The Laundress* (page 27), which he was later to simplify and rework into a lithograph, must be interpreted in a completely different way: namely, as a quickly comprehended, typical, everyday scene. A young laundress, leaning slightly forward and sideward so as to balance the weight of a large basket of laundry, crosses the street. One takes for granted that it is a Parisian street. Under a fashionable upswept coiffure which completely hides the forehead are a nose, mouth, and chin which while not really pretty are not really ugly either. The blouse, gathered at the neck rather like a nightgown, falls over the slim, slumping body. The drawing of the folds in particular and the sober lines of the drawing itself strongly recall statements by Käthe Kollwitz and related draftsmen. Lautrec then summarily crosshatches the long, dark skirt all the way to the bottom of the page, so that the figure seems to emerge from a black pedestal. A laundry wagon, drawn by a rather knobby-legged nag with its feed bag around its neck, is visible behind this compelling figure. Farther down the road a cab moves off. Above it a few general notations indicate the slightly curving façade of a house.

In the July, 1888, issue of *Paris Illustré*, a lithograph based on this drawing was used to illustrate an article on the subject of summer in Paris, written by Émile Michelet.

Die Wäscherin · The Laundress 1888

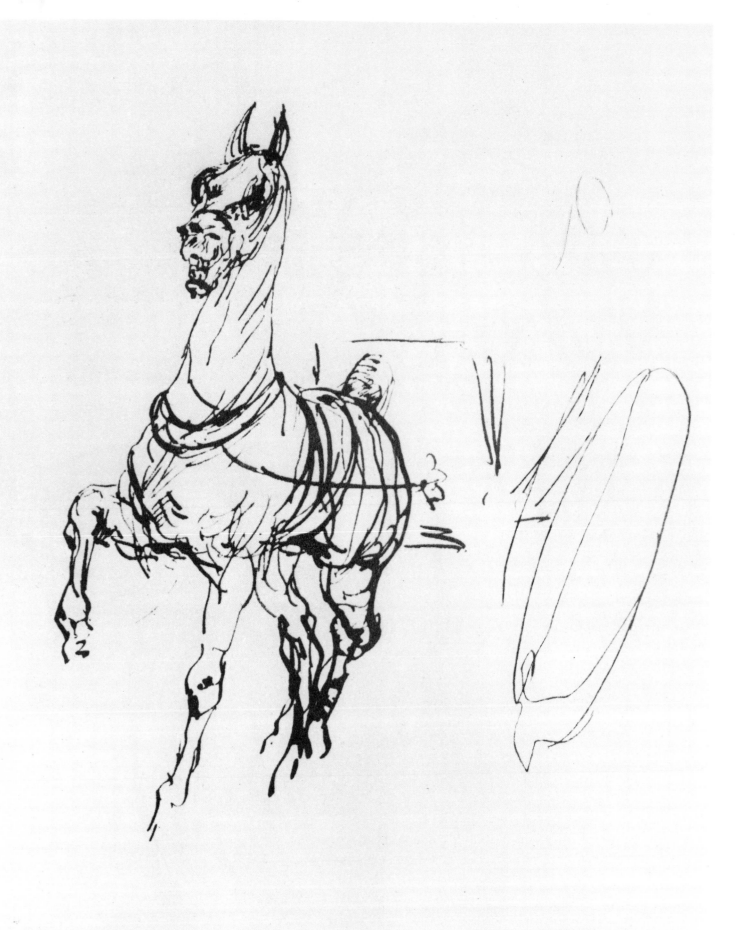

Pferd im Gespann, von vorn · Cantering Horse

Im Moulin Rouge. Auftritt der Cha-U-Kao · La Redoute: Cha-U-Kao's Entrance at the Moulin Rouge on Mardi Gras 1896

Die Goulue und Valentin · La Goulue and Valentin 1894

A careful examination of just what happened when this charcoal drawing was transformed into the final study, in lithographic crayon (plate 3), serves as an example for many similar transformations. Comparison shows that for the lithograph Lautrec cleaned up the scribbling lines, outlined the female figure more boldly, and drew the composition together in a unifying line. The body with the basket seems to swell out behind and follow the rather powerful vertical which runs down the left side of the figure, emphasizing her movement from right to left. Everything has been lightened and the folds of the skirt as well as the basket laths are fleetingly indicated with parallel lines. The paving, which runs into the depth of the picture in fine lines, creates the perspective; cab and laundry cart have become precise areas of dark on either side of the soft, graceful face of the girl, which has been cast even more into shadow. The laundress is now the pillar and the center of the pictorial construction. The nag has become a white horse with blinders. The boulevard on both sides of the scene has come alive. A pedestrian moves away in the background to the right, thus enlarging the space, while to the left, under an awning, a waiter of the café we must imagine to be there busies himself at a table.

Trees, lamps, and façades are briefly noted. There is no sign of social protest here; it is simply a summer morning in Paris, one of Lautrec's many records of the everyday life of his city. What lifts this above the level of mere illustration is the style, which limits itself to the bare essentials. For Lautrec this often meant developing a theme on the basis of a single figure, for he painted and drew according to his talents and his personal desires, retaining his independence from editors and publishers. He mastered the difficult task of grasping the essentials of man and beast in a flashing moment and immortalizing them in a picture. *The Laundress* is full of pertinent statements concerning form, from the head of hair to the fingertips. Their clarity and matter-of-factness is particularly astounding when we remember that the artist

was only twenty-four and had just learned lithography; we are reminded of the style of the young Van Gogh.

Perhaps *The Morning After*, published two years later in the review *Le Courrier Français*, makes all this even clearer. The large drawing for it (plate 1) was done in India ink and blue pencil. The model was Suzanne Valadon, who had posed for other artists (as friends often do) before she herself began to paint. She appears here in the "listless pose of an inveterate drinker" *(dans l'attitude affalée d'une ivrogne invétérée)*, as it was described in 1926 in the first catalogue of his works edited by Lautrec's friend and executor, Maurice Joyant. An even more decisive version of this drawing, with reticulated clusters of lines, is in the Fogg Art Museum in Cambridge, Massachusetts.

The forlorn drinker at a table was a theme of the times, but in this case the intentional cruelty of the representation is soon forgotten and the drawing as an object prevails. Upon close examination one becomes interested in the way in which a multitude of carefully arranged brush strokes form a mighty casque of hair, the bun resting on the nape, which crowns the delicate profile and projects like a thatched roof over the face as the subject gazes into the distance. Single delicate black strokes articulate the drawing like so many threads evenly unwinding from the hair and run through the figure, over the table, the bottle, the glass, even cross the barely indicated emptiness of the restaurant behind, to amass in the shadowy realm under the table in a flourish of parallel strokes of the kind found in *The Laundress*. Again we are reminded of Van Gogh. With the blue pencil he delicately shaded some parts and turned them into cool surfaces.

Lautrec's preference for a mixed technique is evident here as elsewhere. Even in the hasty first sketches from life, often so summary as to be barely recognizable, done at a café concert, on the dance floors of Montmartre, in a bar, at the theater, or at the races, as well as in his first impressions of famous *diseuses* and *chansonnières*, he loved to work simultaneously with ink, chalk, pencil, tempera, and watercolor, less frequently pastel, according to his momentary inspiration. He showed no preference for any of these techniques, except possibly tempera on cardboard. None of these mediums shackled him. The new and unexpected effects produced by his brush as it moved over the picture, now light as a feather, now broad and bold, continuously engaged the observer's attention. Lautrec's genius as a reporter fulfilled itself in his art. Often the strokes of his brush rough in only a single figure or one specific scene, but they always attain their goal and are seldom superfluous; the strokes stop just where the main subject comes to an end. He heightened his painted drawings and sketches with white just as effectively, the touches of white flashing around a figure, taking the form of a diffused spot, or enveloping everything in a stream of light.

All this is particularly evident in the compositions of about 1890 and indicates how Lautrec's feelings toward the world around him never failed to provide him with

varied themes in which a rare creative unrest was united with a taste for novelty. An explanation of the following two pictures, so different in their derivation, is thus made possible: the *Seated Dancer* (plate 2) and *Dr. Péan Operating* (plate 4). Without reserve, leaving the good for the better, impelled into the torrent of a wildly gesticulating human society, amused, touched, Lautrec expressed himself through his models wherever he found them. But this also meant that he actively sought them.

His painting of the young seated dancer is still close to the pictures of women done in the late eighties. But the difference becomes evident if one visualizes the way in which Gavarni, Forain, Alfred Grévin, and even the great Degas himself depicted the world of classical ballet. In place of a condescendingly smiling arrogance and the endless, repetitious group exercises showing perfect mastery of the classical dance, here we have a very human figure of a young dancer, exhausted, breathless, pitifully thin, her head to one side, her strained plain face half turned away, her hands clenched together, her elbows on her thighs, her arms and legs fleshless and pale. Almost mockingly the ruffled costume, with the skirt fanning out like a peacock's tail, flickers whitely here and there in an attempt at gaiety.

Never before had the *rats d'opéra* (young ballet girls) been seen like this, but rather romantically as gallants swarmed around them after the performance and elderly rakes in furs and top hats courted them, invited them, or abducted them into the *chambre séparée*. Lautrec also showed this aspect, more perverse and more true to life, in scenes of an overpowering licentiousness, but at that time it was primarily the "ladies" who were experts in living. Here he painted the "monument of a *balletteuse.*" In another picture he was more descriptively concerned with the great event in the life of the ballet student: the putting on of her first pair of leotards. The essential details so generally sketched around the figure—the sofa,

The Salon in the Rue des Moulins  1894

the wall behind—and the powerful repetitive contours around the excessively slender legs classify this as a colored drawing.

Only where gaiety was justified did Lautrec later exaggerate, caricaturize, rise into the burlesque with a satirical silhouette. The famous *Quadrille Naturaliste* on stage at the Moulin Rouge, the performances of La Goulue and Valentin, the appearance of the male and female clowns, and to a lesser extent the bicycle races, are set apart from that world, including the milieu of the brothels, where tragedy glimmers through the make-up. A single figure might be depicted even here in a disarming, ironic pose, such as the prostitute Rolande, but when this happened it generally belonged to the realm of the cabaret.

The second sketch in this discussion, one among many of this period, draws our interest for quite different reasons. It depicts the then famous surgeon Dr. Péan performing an operation (plate 4). Lautrec gained access to still another field of human activity, studying it thoroughly and at length. At operations where students fainted and Dr. Péan demonstrated an art of surgery which was transmitted in various legendary exaggerations, Lautrec stolidly endured. This world was now also his. The medical student Gabriel Tapié de Céleyran, Lautrec's cousin, friend, and constant companion, as well as a sort of better conscience for the painter when he veered toward debauchery, had just begun his internship with the famous Dr. Péan. And here Lautrec thoroughly explored the operating theater of the Hôpital Saint-Louis in which Dr. Péan strode from operation to operation—and most likely for his time, from masterpiece to masterpiece. He was a heavy man with a mighty head, slicked-down hair, and fashionable full side whiskers, with only a large napkin protecting the dress coat which he wore even while operating. Lautrec often stood so close that he almost seemed to be an assistant surgeon,

but in doing so he found inspiration in the action and in the tension of the surgeon rather than in the operation itself. The patient lying in the foreground has been reduced to a hieroglyph and looks rather like an Oriental temple demon. One surmises his open mouth and his chest rather than recognizing them. Lautrec's account of the operation itself goes no further than the fascinating statement that Dr. Péan might just as well be brooding over a chessboard or meditating at the organ. The singular facial and spiritual nuances which came to the surface here were what interested Lautrec as a painter. From here on Lautrec, like Goya, could say, "I have seen it!" meaning the truth, which could not conceal itself from him. Technically, the light areas spread out over the scene—to use medical terminology—like the frayed ends of a tangle of gauze bandages unrolled over the painter's cardboard.

The brief selection of paintings and drawings presented here, which cover the period until shortly before his death when his artistic powers began to wane, are described more according to their artistic features than their origin and evolution. It therefore seems natural to elaborate at those points where within his restless interests he had discovered something new and which he had then translated into pictorial language. Only ten years are encompassed, within which he created hundreds of sketches, paintings, and lithographs, one right after the other, generally in cycles.

One of the celebrities of the *Belle Époque* was Louise Weber, known as "La Goulue" (The Glutton). Her appearance and style were to influence a whole generation. Originally a laundress, her natural talent soon led her on stage at the Moulin de la Galette, a cabaret on the Butte, where Lautrec first discovered and painted her. Later she danced nightly at the Moulin Rouge, together with Valentin "Le Désossé," (The "Boneless" Man), and they were admired by great crowds of visitors (page 30).

Their fame would have reached us only as legend if the twenty-seven-year-old Lautrec had not been commissioned to make a poster for the concert and dance

*tout les soirs* at the Moulin Rouge to replace a conventional billboard by the old master of lithography, Jules Chéret. This was Lautrec's hour of recognition. His poster was soon affixed to all the advertising pillars and to many walls of Paris. Chéret's innocent and lively gaiety was gone, replaced by an original approach which centered on the leading actors, La Goulue and Valentin. The preparatory sketch (plate 6), about sixty inches high, explains why this poster, which is a translation of line into plane, is so unexpectedly enthralling. Seen from above as a half figure, Valentin, in real life Jacques Renaudin, glides like a mute, grotesque doll from right to left over the foreground of the picture. The play of his gloved hands is emphasized by the artificial pictorial depth which Lautrec boldly borrowed from photography and to whose possibilities Degas had called his attention. The hands are so different in size that they seem to be yards apart. The way in which the faceless figure drifts by—in the poster itself Valentin is nothing but a violet shadow—is Lautrec's astonishing inspiration for concentrating attention on the main figure, La Goulue, whose leg is raised in the air in a cloud of petticoats. Over her severe profile (see also page 62), the famous upswept coiffure towers like an abstract ornament. To the left a ring of gas lights, running out of the picture, are drawn as if Lautrec were floating above them. The dark wall of spectators rises up behind in a half circle. The art of drawing itself was used to sound out the effects of the subsequent poster. With great simplicity Lautrec obtained the spatial depth required by the sweeping movements of these two creatures, who seemed possessed by the dance and who appeared to perform every evening for their own pleasure. From Valentin's front hand, to the firmly planted, delicate shoe of La Goulue, to the barely recognizable spectators with their gay hats shaded in with hatching, the eye proceeds into the depth of the dance hall. No other spatial indications were used. Something more than just an extraordinarily impressive poster was achieved by Lautrec. He exaggerated the ex-

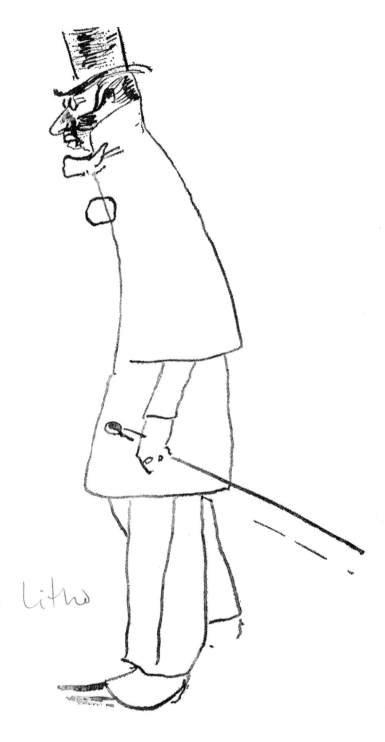

pression and perspective so that even from a distance this "art of the streets" should take the unsuspecting passer-by by storm. A new era in art had begun. From this time on, loss of detail and wealth of color were justified by the impact of simplicity.

This process of inspired simplification, which mirrored Lautrec's own intellectuality and therefore progressively characterized his work, came to the fore whenever publishers and printers assailed the artist for material for reproduction purposes, that is, for lithographs. Illustrations, large posters, music albums, title pages, and announcements of all sorts were in great demand. Although it remained a side line, Lautrec's talent was inadvertently being drawn toward an escalated impact.

Lautrec's study for *The Englishman at the Moulin Rouge* (page 15), probably one of his greatest picture studies, highlights the simplification process in a new way. The painter's friendships corresponded to his social status as well as to his mode of life, and he often reflected his passionate love for England, which he visited repeatedly. *The Englishman at the Moulin Rouge* (plate 7), as this smiling, attentive gentleman in a top hat was called in the subsequent lithograph, was Lautrec's friend from Lincolnshire, a Mr. W. T. Warrener. He survived the painter by almost half a century. What we have here is a portrait, which for Lautrec meant exactness. He made many such portraits of men from his circle of aristocratic friends—blasé or serious, amused, or at least potentially amused.

The study of Warrener was made in 1892. On brown cardboard, the brush has sketched in a basic facial structure with gayly flashing eyes and a cheerful, slightly stub nose, which lends a happy effect, full lips, and a daringly upswept moustache. The head and collar are very simply formulated. Crowning it all sits an elegant top hat which reaches down to just over the eyebrows. The high collar provides a severe base for this face with its lively countenance, kept softly moving by small accompanying strokes, doubled contours, and isolated dark areas which also delineate the outer part of the chin. A new concept of three-dimensionality supervened at this point in the painting process. Lautrec let light fall on the face from the right, lightened the cheek, forehead, and neck with creamy white, advancing precipitously and in broad surfaces against the darkened portions of the face. The light is caught on the cheekbone, the upper lip, and the side of his chin; it is weaker on the nostrils. His ear, however, has been completely obscured by this brightness, as if it were of no importance whatsoever. At the points where dark and light meet, the sketch becomes densest, while the marginal areas are mostly neglected and the opaque yellowish-white streaks of tempera seem to disappear hurriedly under the edges of the top hat and the high collar, above and below the main point of interest.

Many first-hand studies of this kind, in which Lautrec relentlessly remained before his model until he had captured exactly the penetrating expression he was after, can be similarly analyzed. These sketches were then distilled. Although the first impressions remained the basis, they were redone conventionally with their immediacy diminished, as a lithograph or as a painting, finally becoming part of a composition. The finished lithograph (plate 7) to some extent emphasized the man-of-the-world aspect of Warrener's figure as he flirted with two bedizened ladies at the Moulin Rouge. This happened both in the lithograph through the use of ornamental, gently flourishing strokes which emphasized the line and in the painting, where Lautrec painstakingly transmitted the artificially glittering nighttime colors so that he could accurately characterize the routine gaiety of such a small table party. Contemporary photographs of the Folies-Bergère give us an idea of just what these table parties were meant to be; in this case it was for an Englishman out for a good time. No difficulties present themselves for Lautrec as far as form is concerned, regardless of the number of overlappings he might invent.

It seems to have been in Lautrec's nature to dedicate himself completely to the personalities who peopled the idle world of entertainment and came to life when night held sway. But it was just as true that he abandoned his

favorite models as soon as their star began to set. Many owed their quick rise to fame to Lautrec, who prepared their great moment and raised them up to the Olympus of art. How modest by comparison are the fruits of our own artistic harvest, where artists no longer see their fellow human beings and no longer transmit them to us. As a result our knowledge about them or the way they saw their friends, their patrons, and their enemies, in short their contemporaries, dies with them.

Aristide Bruant, a former railroad employee who wrote songs in his spare time, founded the cabaret the Mirliton in 1885, when he was thirty-four. He himself appeared there, eccentrically dressed in a black velvet suit, red shawl, cape, broad-brimmed floppy hat, and short boots. He treated the arriving guests, a charmed metropolitan public, with the brash outspokenness of a rustic, both in his mordant songs and in his barrage of derogatory remarks, the *engueulades*. When the drawing power of the Mirliton began to wane he switched to the café concert Les Ambassadeurs near the famous old Hôtel Crillon on the Place de la Concorde at the foot of the Champs Elysées. The name was derived from the fact that it was next to the hotel where ambassadors stayed. Still later Bruant went to the Eldorado.

All of Lautrec's notations concerning Bruant clearly reveal that he was an outstanding personality, a unique type something like the great *diseuse* of his time, Yvette Guilbert. Lautrec unfailingly set his sights on Bruant and designed posters (particularly for Les Ambassadeurs) so novel in their simplification and so striking that Bruant refused to go on stage unless they were posted. This was in 1893–94, when the zenith of his career had already passed.

This brilliant poseur who at the beginning had thundered out songs for two and a half francs and a glass of wine was caught by Lautrec as a maliciously smiling cynic, glancing over his shoulder. The posters intensified this with an exactly calculated mimicry, but the black-and-white lithograph (plate 9) and its preparatory drawing (plate 8) are richer in nuances. A great comedian was discovered here. His crude, burlesque style had brought him fame and he acted the part to the full. Leaning against the wings, half turned away yet still turning back to the audience, presumptuous and sly, he savors the effect of his appearance on the scene. The corners of his mouth and the eyebrows are drawn in opposing directions; above a sneering nose the appraising eyes are half closed. The preparatory drawing for the lithograph is a masterpiece in its own right. Here Lautrec was still lavish in his use of contour strokes for the arms and scarf, and for the brim of the hat and the hair. He had unfailingly hit the mark although the ensuing lithograph was to define it more precisely by developing light and dark areas, the face and scarf alone standing out as light areas. There are no longer any reminiscences of Van Gogh in this drawing. Soft, long, thick, sweeping strokes move up and down the sheet. Although one looks in vain for anything comparable in the French art of the time, rendering of this sort is to be found in the art of Edvard Munch.

The themes of the paintings and drawings of 1892–93 were generally drawn from the world of the café concert. *Conférenciers*, merrymakers, singers, and above all dancers and *diseuses*—that is, the cabaret stars—were represented as no other painter was ever to equal. Unlike La Goulue, who was unique, they were often cultured as well as brilliant, such as the enigmatic Jane Avril (plate 11), who even took part in a Parisian representation of *Peer Gynt*.

Lautrec's studies of the dancer Jane Avril are representative of a long series of celebrities of the "minor arts." She belonged to the *Quadrille Quartette* in the Moulin Rouge, which Lautrec set down in a gayly impudent poster prepared for their London appearance. Here we have the troop of Mademoiselle Églantine, all in white, with frothy feather hats and wildly waving black-stockinged legs. The rather saucy, screwed-up faces with their blinking, flirtatious eyes are anything but pretty.

They again typify Lautrec's tendency to exaggerate into the grotesque, absolutely lacking that saccharine charm attributed them by his contemporaries. In compensation, Lautrec sided with his models even when he mocked them. He provided them with life and credibility. The pages and paintings dedicated to Jane Avril reveal just this, even though the results were just about as much as she could take.

In 1893 Lautrec sketched the then twenty-five-year-old young woman (page 61), whose father was said to have belonged to the Italian nobility, at the Jardin de Paris, where she had made her debut. This sketch is a study for the famous poster (page 21) discussed above.

Jane Avril was nicknamed "La Mélinite," which means more or less "high explosive." If we can trust Lautrec, she liked to pass herself off as slightly mad in her stage appearances and bizarre in her dance movements. The *Quadrille Quartette* poster in which she affords more comic relief than a startled flamingo hints at this. She was extravagant and eccentric in her dress, and displayed a droll seriousness which made her seem something like a philosopher on stage. Lautrec often depicted her in a pensive, even meditative, mood (page 25). Sometimes she appeared to be whispering short monologues as an accompaniment to her storklike dances.

The free study (page 61) for the poster can be considered a self-sufficient work of art. It seems almost chiseled out of the brown cardboard. The grand orange-colored sweep of the skirt enlivens the picture; the long black gloves and stockings add a sombre tone. Jane Avril wears an openwork blouse and a towering black-and-white hat over her reddish-blond hair. This must be seen in the light of Lautrec's propensity for understanding, for transmitting his impression of this hook-shaped creature with his own peculiar style of brushwork. The silhouette of the foot on the ground as well as of the one moving through the air are outlined in opaque white much the way in which a rough drawing prepared for the engraver has been corrected and retouched. While Lautrec, as was his habit, captured only a single moment of the stalking, burlesquing movement of the dance, this time a cursory transience left him unsatisfied, and like a miniaturist he dotted in flounces, laces, embroidery, and feathers with a fine brush—now light areas, now dark—even indicating the meshes of the silk stockings. He was attentive to the way the silk skirt fell over the arm with which Jane Avril lifted her out-flung leg in a pose of overpowering comedy, which later proved to be the culminating point of all his inspirations. Over the figure, the face, illuminated from the footlights, with artificially shadowed eyes and pursed lips, discharges all the mockery it was capable of.

After this, Lautrec's style changed very little, except perhaps for an occasional bounding of areas with color so as to stress the pictorial character of particular inventions. An insight into what went on in his mind is possible during the period when he created the circus series, that is in 1899, when he was ill. They provide a panorama of his visual experiences, and for the physician they prove his rehabilitation as a sound human being. But his vital powers were already broken. These scenes, projected from memory, have become acute and overexact. Lautrec's beloved reality of the arena is seen as though through the wrong end of a telescope, and the almost academic refinement deprives it of its freshness and spontaneity. Here, Lautrec was trying once more to be Lautrec.

For an understanding of his artistic procedure it is useful to compare the study of Jane Avril looking at fresh proof (plate 11) with the later lithograph used as a cover for *L'Estampe originale* published by the *Journal des Artistes*, a print in black, white, and color showing Jane Avril and an old printer at his handpress. Lautrec's never-failing process of simplification from the drawing to the printed image is clearly discernible. There is something almost painful in the way Lautrec forsook the nuances which abound in his paintings. In the lithograph the slender, unequivocal line had to render all that which had been qualified as space in the study: a cloudy half shadow, a delicate smudge near the eye and another hovering near the brow, and the darkened area of the rather long face. In its translation into a lithograph (plate 10) this loving immersion into the elusive air of Jane Avril's character yields to a carefully balanced framework of fine, vibrating lines of equal importance moving from her cape to the sheet of paper she holds before her, to the printing press. For all its exactness there is an ingenious abandon in its description, including even old Père Cotelle, who had worked many years for Lautrec's printer Ancourt. His grateful disciple here immortalized him in all his vitality, his famous greasy black kepi included. Whether in its black-and-white state prior to the addition of lettering (reproduced here) or in the later version in which pale colors dissolve the drawing, this page is a milestone in the history of lithography, which was then starting its victorious ascent. The impression provided by the delicate figure of Jane Avril in the final color lithograph can be compared only to the pictorial aspect of the Japanese color wood-block print with its transparent tones and the wonderful intentional suppression of spatial depth. Even her face is like that of a white-powdered Japanese woman. The vitality of a highly sensitive face which comes to the fore in the study was withdrawn behind the mask of a newly discovered style.

The immediacy of an unconstrained encounter speaks out of each of Lautrec's portraits and each of his studies. Wherever Lautrec appeared the seriousness of his artistic intent swept away all prejudice, giving him access even to the artists, dressing rooms where they made up for their stage appearances—nervous, joking, improvising, or seeking adulation—where the effects of a witticism or a new idea were tried out, and where the last thing they wanted was to sit as a model. And yet it was here that the phenomenal mixture of make-believe, buf-

to say about him. No flowers blossomed on the café tables that Lautrec saw, sunlight had nothing to seek in the boudoirs he painted, and the only sky blue was the canopy of a four-poster bed.

In addition to the blustering Bruant he discovered the amusing Caudieux, famous for his good humor and for the difficulty he had in looking down at his shoes. Caudieux appeared at Les Ambassadeurs, at the Eldorado, and at the Petit-Casino; he sang catchy tunes and was lord of the stage with his scooping arm movements and the gayest leaps imaginable (page 63). Lautrec also stood next to him as, half dressed, he powdered his face before his stage entrance (plate 15)—and a formidable task it was, as a large sketch in Albi shows. Caudieux again appeared in a poster of 1893 hastening toward the audience in his dress coat, his tails flying, and above, a rosy, sleek face with a tiny mouth. The area between eye and ear is flooded with warm pink. On the poster the starved prompter can be seen at his feet closed in his green box, the exact counterpart of Caudieux.

In the tempera sketch illustrated here (plate 15) Lautrec has made particular note of the amiable quality of the face and its relaxed expression. To achieve this he needed nothing more than the facial form, the line of the nose, the smiling eyes and mouth, retouched with white. Thickened brush strokes delineate the hair and neck more sharply, and from the head the lines run down into the corpulent body. The hand holding the powder puff is treated summarily. Neither a dressing-room mirror nor any other object distracts the eye. Once Lautrec had captured this fleeting instant in the life of the resting comedian, he then represented him completely dressed, on stage, where this moment of private enchantment had vanished.

The art of this painter and draftsman reached from the almost idyllic to the heroic—to the representation of human drama. The newspaper *Le Matin* ordered a poster to advertise the memoirs of Abbé Faure. The title of the

foonery, and tenacity was to be found which often enabled Lautrec to strike root. His skill soon became evident and allowed him to follow his goal undisturbed. His vision of beauty and truth was sufficiently convincing that he could avoid the necessity for flattery.

This great truth to life eliminated conventions. Lautrec drew, painted, designed on stone, as the gods had intended him to do. If he had abandoned this path, other worlds in which he would have had to throttle the originality of his keen observation might have become the objects of his way of seeing and today we would have little

poster is *Au Pied de l'Échafaud* ("At the Foot of the Scaffold"). The rough draft (plate 5) is a veritable thunderstorm of lines. A condemned man, his hands bound behind his back and his shirt open, leans rigidly into the scene from the right. Even more telling than the distorted face is the wonderfully horrifying way in which Lautrec conveyed the shivering of the wretch with a milky-blue color accompanying the cold, gloomy sunlight.

The man's distorted face is turned upward toward the guillotine, which looms menacingly in the foreground. The lower semicircle seems ready and waiting for his neck. To the right is the vague form of the executioner in a top hat; his ominous hand rests heavily on the shoulder of the victim. Surrounding them, the empty space is mercilessly bounded at some distance by a dark, shadowy mounted phalanx. While the scene as a whole recalls the realism found in his picture of Dr. Péan operating, it is even closer to depictions such as Daumier's mighty *Ecce Homo* in the Folkwang Museum in Essen, where the broad, brown brush strokes seem to move within the picture like ghosts. On the whole one's mind turns to related depictions in French painting since Géricault. Lautrec's idea is new. Only individual parts—the neck and head of the condemned man, the figure of the executioner, and, paler, the mounted cordon—have been dipped in color and extended, formless and ghostlike, in glacial blue, blackish purple, and dead green. The rest of the picture has been deigned only a few pertinent short strokes of the brush, as if he couldn't get the subject done quickly enough. The finished poster had to put across the drama and make its subject matter clear. The scene of the finished work is dominated by the rigid oxblood-red letters especially of *Le Matin*, and the guillotine is of the same color. The victim in the white shirt, more recognizably chained, conceals his grimace in a faded green; the executioner has become slightly caricaturized as a grouchy individual. This is not at all far from the later *Simplizissimus*. In front of the now black mounted platoon a peevish-looking priest makes his appearance, as if he were almost an afterthought: Abbé Faure himself, who as La Roquette's chaplain had accompanied thirty-eight condemned persons to the foot of the guillotine.

Meant as they were to be viewed in everyday life, many scenes were similarly changed in their passage from the original sketches to the posters—or the "people's gallery" as they were called, since they were seen on every street corner. But any loss in detail and authentic artistic annotation was compensated for by the unprecedented impressiveness of this new pictorial language. The man in the street, who had never before related an artistic event to what happened in the world around him, regardless of what it communicated, was confronted with an art that was abbreviated in execution, color, and context. For the first time he began to read pictures.

Lautrec's biographers report that in the subsequent years his intellectual interests and life ideals changed. He visited the attractions of Montmartre less frequently and was driven instead to explore the heart of this quarter, to seek out the prostitutes and the brothels themselves, the *maisons closes*. He lived for some time in the most luxurious one in Rue des Moulins, since the owner had asked him to decorate the *salon* with pictures. Lautrec accepted this commission with joy and painted a series portraying the girls of the house.

Unwittingly he found himself in the role of a naturally accepted companion to these girls and women. He experienced their everyday life, he portrayed it in a way never equaled before or after and with perfect objectivity. His sensitivity for the ever-persistent remains of warm humanity, which these creatures also had, enabled him to do that. It was precisely this closeness that toned down the implication of depravity, which Lautrec fails to report. Other artists, such as George Grosz and Otto Dix, and before them Jules Pascin, have taken prostitution as a theme on which to pass judgment, either glorifying it or damning it.

Lautrec was the center of attraction as he painted a

The Clowness Cha-U-Kao (detail) 1895

series of medallions in the *salon* with portraits of the ladies. They sat for him, and without any embarrassment he was made an eyewitness to their life. As an artist and as a confidant, as well as a person who aroused compassion and who was therefore himself in need of friendship, he represented it without coarse or dissolute features. He was always true to his inborn distinction, which rejected moralizing even from afar. In George Rouault's remarkable representations of prostitutes there is always a sense of dark foreboding, however lifelike the shadowy figures with vacantly staring faces and heavy peasant limbs may be. It is always a Saul who paints here.

Lautrec approached this region of life without taking sides. The pictures and sketches which were done in the brothels appear before us mute and introverted—a treasure-trove for writers. But for anyone who is interested in Lautrec's style, they are further evidence of a prodigiously sure eye, in which not a single moment betrays any trace of boredom.

At least as many pictures followed in this series, which also includes illustrations, as had come before, and for once his subject was thoroughly dealt with. Lautrec's inventions in the *mise en scène* of such motifs once again reveal the whole range of his talent and the extraordinary power of his imagination.

The double portrait of the owners of a brothel (plate 16) in the Toulouse-Lautrec Museum, Albi, lifts the theme almost to the level of burlesque. Painted in 1893, *Monsieur, Madame, and Dog* are presented to the observer seated on a red sofa. Behind them is a mirror with a blurred reflection of the room. This would be simply a colored drawing were it not for the solid areas of color which surround both figures. Monsieur is the image of feigned inertia with an expressionless face, a disagreeable broad-bridged nose, small puffy cheeks, and a straggly mustache, while on his forehead lies a lock of hair combed down from the center of his balding head. Lautrec has here characterized a dingy variety of the humble citizen,

neither flattering him nor exaggerating. The hand which holds the cigarette could easily cover an entire face.

The face that Lautrec encountered must actually have been like this. It is inconceivable that he should have purposely searched for an expression of criminality, and it is far too serious for a caricature. The same can be said for Madame, who turns left, out of the picture, which in a sense makes her physiognomy unrecognizable, for the face has been transformed into an unbroken series of flourishes and counterflourishes: stub nose, puffy eyes, receding chin, and topped by a pitiful head of hair whose thin locks are trained over the forehead. In her lap she holds, encircled by a formless hand, a lively little dog with pointed ears. An expressionless silence reigns between the figures. Vertical strokes of varying thickness define the clothing as of the department-store variety, light material which covers a person both cheaply and amorphously. Lautrec represented the two human beings as apparently lethargic but actually attentively observing the course of the events they manipulate. Maupassant was not as successful in his rendering of this truth when he described the Maison Tellier.

Let us anticipate Lautrec's finale on this theme: the picture *The Salon in the Rue des Moulins* (page 33), which was done in 1894. The picture, about fifty-one inches wide, is one of his largest and is painted and composed throughout, the sum of all his sketches and a faultless example of Lautrec's mature style, which is also in the style of the painting of the time. If it had been hung in the Louvre rather than in Albi this picture would long ago have testified to Lautrec's painting, for here his form emerges pure.

Studies for *The Salon* were collected for months, and it was preceded by a rather pale pastel sketch. Then in his studio Lautrec painted the classic "unrelated togetherness" of prostitutes waiting for clients in an Oriental sort of *salon*. Madame, prim and prudishly dressed, looks out of the picture—she alone—as if to size up the observer with an inscrutable look. Words can hardly do justice to the mixture of conciliation and indolence expressed by the figure sitting in the foreground. Considering her extended bare arm, her hand grasping the carelessly drawn up green-stockinged leg, and the way the figure tips slightly backward as she leans on the raspberry-red bolster of the sofa, she seems to guide the eye automatically into this pompously decorated room in which other girls in extreme décolleté are arranged like wax figures around a green fluted column. The column, together with the reflections in the background, recalls the stage sets which Lautrec painted, rather than a real room.

But let us return to Lautrec's point of departure in this thoroughly studied composition. With her negligently comfortable pose the girl in the light dress in the foreground provides a pull into the depth of this overdecorated room, but with a certain hesitance so that the surface development of the picture is not neglected. The dark, straight line of the extended leg holds the picture fast in the lower-right corner and continues the line of the bare arm. The back of this attractive figure with yellowish-red hair and a friendly, well-cut profile indicates the center of the picture. From her to the stiff Madame dressed in mauve, out of whose bony face green eyes seek to nail fast the beholder, then to a full figure in an unrelenting front view whose bosom is barely covered by a dark dress. The figural composition then curves around the porcelain-green column to two seated women, neither of whom is particularly reticent with her charms. Compared with the faces in the right half of the picture, theirs are more caricatured. (In preparatory studies Lautrec had permitted himself an even greater freedom.) Here it is a matter of carefully focused draftsmanship and the identification of each single person, the inmates of the Rue des Moulins, who are known by name: the pretty Mireille is in the foreground; in the back sits the buxom Rolande. At the right a more schematic standing figure is half cut off by the edge of the picture so that her dishabille is minimized.

Space is not particularly important here as elsewhere. It does not absorb the waiting forms, but only responds to the individual figures set in varying planes of depth, who loom larger in the pictorial space than they would on center stage. The violet couch occupies a great deal of space. The emptiness of the lower left portion of the picture, in which a veritable landscape of sofas and bolsters unfolds, emphatically leads back to the suppressed gestures of the women themselves, who look past each other, who do not laugh, and yet who do not seek to conceal themselves reciprocally.

When this important undertaking in all its earnestness was finished and this incomparable exhibition piece of a brothel had been set up, when Lautrec had laid aside his brush, a photograph was taken in which the painter, as usual in hat and vest, smilingly observes the picture from one side, his hands in his pants pockets. On the other side of the picture one of his models, completely nude and with a lance in her hand, also observes the picture. Probably the painter intended with such an apparently frivolous jest to smother any budding sentimentality concerning this lost world and its creatures.

This picture, which is the sum of all his exact observations in the brothels, was preceded by a period of feverish activity in which he did not even stop to go out for meals, but ate together with his models while producing his quick and penetrating studies. He investigated his subject matter thoroughly, somewhat the way in which living animals in a zoo are studied, freely offering themselves and depicted in a way of which they are unaware and which lies completely beyond their comprehension.

The results were studies of such intimacy and such a natural corporal beauty that the restrictions of the milieu are forgotten. This is revealed most clearly in the lithographic series *Elles*, one of the outstanding works of modern graphics, where a specific environment has been elevated to the level of great art. Through intimacy Lautrec, a kind friend, attained a greater style. There is no other explanation for this series of sketches of the everyday life of prostitutes.

Marcelle Lender Doing the Bolero in "Chilpéric"  1895

A few examples from this area of Lautrec's production, which was still to conquer and plumb other spheres until his power came to an end, serve to highlight his talent to proceed from the given. At times hastily sketching, at others touched by an expression, he directed his attention from one to the other of the women, characterized them acutely, depicted them lovingly.

The tempera study on cardboard of a reclining woman with her arms crossed above her head (plate 14)—resting and not sleeping—is perhaps the most universal of his artistic statements about individuals. The youthfully slender body is bathed in light only around the head, arms, and one breast. Hair and clothing, depicted with curved sweeping lines, are merely an airy network of lines. Once again Lautrec has set his strong contours unfailingly right, just where they really count, framing the face and darkly encircling the armpit and shoulder, which are turned toward the observer. They are more than sufficient to indicate what occupied Lautrec here, what it was that he wanted to solve—reclining repose. This is shown in the quiet, withdrawn face, the silent center of a pentagon formed by the arms and torso, with the color flaring and waning. Yet the indication of light on the raised arm is so free that the white brush strokes themselves take over the function of contours. Lautrec was at this time thirty years old.

The great number of Lautrec's drawings which have been preserved in the form of menus, greetings to friends, small remembrances of episodes and escapades are a kind of accessory to the closed series of his themes. They are often so abbreviated that their usually ironic content can only be guessed at. These "stenograms" constitute another region of his seeing and his experiencing of the world. Here he is the *grand seigneur*, expressing mockery of his peers in drawing. His caricatures were not meant to call forth the laughter of the public. Scribbled in pen and ink, they range from actual derision to annotations of human beings and animals, studies of facial expression,

ironic self-portraits, to completely painted pictures where a touch of mockery can nevertheless be found, even though it may be as little as that which catches the appearance of the girl Rolande in *The Salon*.

The same may be said for *The Tattooed Woman* (page 35) in her pale blue chemise with a red sash and a ribbon in her hair. Forthrightness is allowed here. In this dressing scene Lautrec has overstated the main figure with her buffalolike profile and full neck, the powerful tattooed arm hanging down at her side, as well as the assisting figure behind her. The tattooed woman at her dressing-table mirror is emphasized all the more by the gaunt, draped figure, who stands behind her like a blue shadow arranging her sash. Long, narrow slits of eyes and mouth flash dangerously from her lean face. Such overdrawing is not rare with Lautrec and is better known in his lithographs, where the accuracy of the portrait is diminished by bold simplification. But that is not the case here, where the one quality promotes the other, and the laughter is not diabolic. Masquerade was one of the laws of this life, a fact which Lautrec always expressed through a certain unrelatedness of the figures to each other, except for those scenes where human beings were not lined up and concentrated on "pleasure for all." Lautrec found quieter tones when people were turned to each other, like his two lovers in the environment of Lesbians to whom he dedicated an entire cycle of pictures. In some ways they are related to Degas. Free as they may be, there is nothing offensive in them, for they are first of all works of art with the subject matter relegated to second place. Also, with Lautrec the theme always falls into the realm of question and exchange, and what he produced were double portraits more than anything else, even though they were of reclining and seated female figures, concealing more than they revealed and leaving the subject matter in suspension. Whatever the case, none of these depictions approaches the homage to Eros found in Courbet's picture *Friends* in the Petit Palais in Paris.

Lautrec's models were of course also the poor, common

girls, set on paper with their round faces—"pretty faces" with short noses and a slightly reproachful expression, which was one of their distinguishing features. Lautrec, when he appeared before them as a man, tore them out of their small security so that he could paint them and conquer them as an artist, a profession of which the Madame had perhaps heard only vaguely. Lautrec transmitted what he found there with the accuracy of an unbiased journalist, to which he added his skill.

In *The Two Friends* (plate 17) Lautrec describes the subject in his usual way with just a few concentrated areas of lines. But he also constructs a kind of nest around the two girls. The overlapping gestures, the bent heads and bodies, and the intermingling of their wraps, couple them together. They form a quiet, harmonious unit, the life of each one depending on the other. Their faces are stated briefly: full lips, vacant eyes which, unlike those in *The Salon* picture, have nothing to detect, for here nothing leads beyond the two figures themselves. Lautrec, familiar with all their joys and needs, saw their pains both large and small. The crowding here does not suggest any uncertainty of spatial feeling. The essential human quality which Lautrec was first to express so completely was later taken as a model by twentieth-century artists, especially the Fauves and the Expressionists.

The portrait *Marcelle* of 1894 (page 39), an homage to one of his favorite models, betrays the involvement of a sentiment similar to love. Lautrec, the friend and generous visitor of houses of ill repute, ungrudging in his gifts and capable of finding, of creating, of reaping the high points of life at this sordid level, probably also won the hearts of these creatures. Here he did not encounter the distrustful glances of the provincials who stopped in at the bars or the offensive laughter of some thoughtless individual as he did along the Atlantic coast where Lautrec, being a passionate swimmer, went in summer. Here in these houses he had nothing to fear. Only here could his

need for warmth and love find response, for offensiveness was excluded.

Marcelle in profile appears bold, aware, practiced in pleasure and well acquainted with all the arts of Eve, just the opposite of the graceful Hélène Vary whom Lautrec had repeatedly painted six years before when she was only an inexperienced girl of eighteen. One is still tempted, however, to turn to that early classic profile portrait; it is our first indication of how early Lautrec cemented himself in the art of characterization. In both portraits the painter's passion belonged to the work itself.

How exact from forehead to chin is the likeness of Marcelle, a child of the people. How perfectly the brow has been drawn, the flared nostrils, and the corner of the mouth where the vertical line closes off the knowing lips. How much a whole is the head. There is something adventurous in the faint red on the nose, mouth, and ear. One could almost speak exhaustively of the coloring without mentioning the jacket thrown loosely over the shoulders, its light tone like that of the breast formulated by a few slashing brush strokes, nor even of the blue of the bedspread visible behind her face. And we have not yet mentioned the wild hair, which falls over the forehead, over the temples, and boldly onto the nape. There are no compromises. The picture is a masterpiece from the first to the last stroke, and the last stroke was soon put down. But not before the essentials had been grasped so masterfully that it seems as though Lautrec had practiced what was hardest of all, making a human face into a mirror of all the emotions dwelling behind its façade. And all of this he accomplished with a minimum of crossed lines.

The study of a girl putting on her stockings (page 43), one of the most rapid sketches in this series, has retained a more graceful charm. In Lautrec's studies from the nude his love of truth generally came to the fore, whether in the representation of overlarge feet or in the involuntarily comic rendering of the back of a boyish girl caught unaware as she dresses. Comedy can also be the subject matter, even here. In this respect the basic studies, the primary pictorial inspirations always left the strongest impression, even if they did not achieve the rank of later, more finished pictures.

Momentary inspiration should not, however, be used to classify these studies, as the colored drawing of the girl putting on her stockings proves. From the time of Lautrec's biographer Joyant, this drawing has been reproduced in every large work on Lautrec, and there is a reason for this. With its simple contours and with the flashes of color which illuminate portions of the figure—fox-colored hair, sky-blue shirt thrown around the neck and shoulders, white for the breasts and hip, and indications of olive green for the stockings—the subject reaches back to the point where Lautrec raised a figure, in this case in the liberty of the almost nude, from the dead brown of the cardboard into a dimensional reality. Only in the head and shoulders did he use a naturalistic color rendering.

A related study is that of *Mademoiselle Lucie Bellanger* (plate 22) done in 1896. The upper part of a full, comely person is shown partially undressed. It is drawn in outlines, and is rather reminiscent of the *Woman in Bed* (plate 14), although in finer contours, as if the study were to serve as a preparation, in its imposing earthiness, for his lithographic series *Elles*. Only the head and bosom of the figure are more or less finished. The arm, slip, and blouse are designated with a few light and dark brush strokes. The hand already lies outside his field of interest. The way in which Lautrec concentrated his artistic energies in a fleeting profile until he achieved a portrait likeness, thereby illustrating his method of finding form, is extraordinary.

All these studies are small in size, reducing what is represented to the proportions of a large drawing, whereas the study for the head of Marcelle is half life-size.

These studies, which comprise the material which a painter must collect, have survived thanks to the care of his friends. Had they fallen into the hands of censors, they would have been lost to us. The Toulouse-Lautrec Museum in Albi still exhibits what the Louvre, on behalf of the Luxembourg Museum in Paris, once indignantly rejected. But this was after Lautrec's time.

Lautrec prepared his own early end by imbibing all sorts of "poisons" of Montmartre in generous quantities. Physically he managed to survive another five years. Up to just before the turn of the century his work—interrupted by trips to England, to the seaside, to Spain and Portugal, but no farther—was characterized by an increasingly rapid sequence of themes and spheres, often of completely opposing kinds.

He loved change and it kept him alive, that is, through painting. Themes were more than an exterior façade; they reached into his interior as the shifting stimuli of his innermost self, serving to overcome his dwarfism, to rise up to the occasion when the flippant tongue of the queen of Montmartre, the great *diseuse* Yvette Guilbert (page 62) seemed to prohibit an approach by the painter. From its inception this encounter was attuned to *esprit* alone. Yet Lautrec was not to paint a single portrait of this woman who has survived to our time only through his lithographs and posters. In trying to capture her spirit and her indolent way of singing risqué chansons in a picture, Lautrec completely sacrificed the grace which old photographs attempt to put across.

He had to surpass Yvette, whom he considered great, in intellectual stature; he had to stop playing the part of patron and buffoon; he had to conquer her female vanity before he was able to sketch her as he saw her when she performed at the Moulin Rouge and at the Divan Japonais. Even though years before Lautrec had shown her in the background of the poster for the Divan Japonais—

59

albeit without head—only in 1894 had she reached the top and thus furnished him with a new subject.

The Museum of Art in Providence preserves the lithograph corrected in watercolor in which Yvette Guilbert was translated most boldly of all into Lautrec's language. The preparatory sketch in Albi (plate 13) does not exactly start with the human quality of the figure either. For her performances Yvette wore a short green dress and long black gloves, her make-up was completely personal, almost clownlike, and her hair was cut short. In itself this would all be pleasant enough if her performance did not exclude any possibility of mildness. She addressed herself to a demanding audience, and when her mouth finally closed, her naughty words still hung in the air. But she clung to the curtain as here, bowed and merged, like a human shadow, into the props set up around her.

Lautrec thus precisely indicated the position of the adversaries and where blade met blade. If this sketch was preparatory to one of the lithographs in that famous portfolio whose entrance into the world was sanctioned by Yvette Guilbert when she signed the title page, it testifies to a rare determination on the part of Lautrec to adhere to a style which was new to him and for which he was not again to find an adequate model. This human hieroglyph with the face of a yellow-haired castle spook and vampirelike arms is no longer a flesh and blood human being. It is the incarnation of the cabaret itself, the voice of nocturnal wisdom, frightening the Babbitts and delighting the sophisticate, that has taken form in the almost-human figure of Yvette Guilbert.

With the trace of corporality which Lautrec left her and which gave her the quality of a Dulcinea del Tobosa (the misty figure who enraptured Don Quixote), she was the epitome of all that Montmartre meant for Paris and the world. In her, human wit triumphed. There was no longer a question of beauty or ugliness.

Yvette Guilbert lived until 1944, and thus her last traces were slow to vanish. She toured throughout the world and was more than just the symbol of Montmartre.

She was a sublime journalist who made the ghost of the *Belle Époque* live for those who still wanted to accept the remote wonder of the nineties.

Other versions in Lautrec's pictorial language fail to mitigate what *Yvette Guilbert Taking a Curtain Call* offers. Each time he depicted her like this: motionless, savoring a word, whispering something unutterable, with her black-gloved arms and her hands, which were even more expressive in the black gloves, raised at her side, for the words reached to her very fingertips.

Yvette Guilbert's long gloves (plate 12), the most famous gloves in the world in their time, were immortalized by Lautrec in this brilliant sketch. The interment of an epoch, with their blackness falling from step to step, this sketch was used for a lithograph and appeared on the jacket of the album dedicated to her. With the black gloves emphasized here and there by white retouching, the sketch reveals them as veritable glove beings. They are finally free, rid of the framework of bones and skin which they had enclosed. And lying there they seem like the silent ghost of the *fin-de-siècle*, a long shadow as of a bon mot which has vanished in thin air. The appropriate word picture can be no other than a reversal of the story of Peter Schlehmiehl, a well-known figure in German literature who sold his shadow to the devil. Here, only his shadow remains.

This abbreviation lifted Lautrec into the sphere of the great figures of painting. Not even the Nabis could take leave of the world of things more imperturbably than this, or give form with their colors and shapes to that other world which was exclusively theirs.

The year 1894 was productive for Lautrec and one in which he also took greater liberties in his treatment of surfaces. His picture of his cousin, Gabriel Tapié de Céleyran (page 47) is reminiscent of Gauguin. A constant companion and friend, he had introduced Lautrec to the milieu of the great surgeon, Dr. Péan. The painter always needed someone close by and as a result Tapié was also often his model. In this lovely picture, narrow and high

Melinit-Tanz der Jane Avril · Jane Avril Dancing 1893

Henri de Toulouse-Lautrec, Selbst-Karikatur
Henri de Toulouse-Lautrec, Self-Caricature  1896

La Goulue  ·  La Goulue

Yvette Guilbert  ·  Yvette Guilbert  1893

Die Schauspielerin Marcelle Lender  ·  Marcelle Lender, the Actress

Caudieux, im Petit-Casino tanzend  ·  Caudieux Dancing at the Petit-Casino  1893

Madame Poupoule bei der Toilette · Woman at her Toilet: Mme. Poupoule 1898

and with finished surfaces, he is shown as he leaves the theater, thoughtfully pacing along, a fashionable figure as far as clothing, hair style, and top hat are concerned. But who ever saw a dandy so solidly nailed fast to the fiery red floor with a gait which contradicts the nobility of the composition? One leg has its large foot set firmly on the floor, while the other, with a rolling movement of the trouser leg is still far from ready to move into the next step. A persistently singular humor has been infused into this figure. It seems as if his legs were playing a joke on this thoughtful young gentleman, dignified though he is. But it is just this unique gait which seems to set these autonomous dark feet in motion and which makes the figure impressive. Reserved, shadowless, the figure rises up, caught only at intervals by the cloaked personages and the open loge farther to the left, through which can still be seen the distant stage proceedings, glowing red, and parts of the proscenium. Edvard Munch's contemporary full-figure portraits of men are more severely sculptural, like painted statues. But this statue moves, paces off the underlying red floor in its own unique gait, sunk in thought, a willing and indefatigable model for his admired cousin. He smoothed Lautrec's path and after his death, together with Joyant, saw to it that his native town of Albi received its great heritage. For some years the Toulouse-Lautrec Museum collection traveled around the world and delighted the eyes of many people.

Tapié is more than a figure of the times, and the burning red floor sets this rare full-figure portrait on a level with contemporary European painting. Besides Gauguin one thinks of Bonnard and Vuillard. Lautrec's draftsmanlike conception of the motif and his way of painting are not as obvious as theirs. But here we are dealing with a rare pictorial liberty, even where the blue-black, darkened by the underlying red, advances toward the observer. Only a few years later August Macke and the German Expressionists were to use such wide-stepping positions in their portraits, which often seemed purposely posed, unconcerned with whatever the empirical spatial depth of European painting might still count for. They turned Lautrec's flatness, which was generally indebted to the Far East, into a tilted depth; in other words they put seven-league boots on their striding figures. Lautrec's quiet sense of humor in his depiction of his cousin Tapié was seriously elevated to the level of a creative principle.

In the last years of his life Lautrec's works became immeasurably varied. The life of Paris, seen from a café, in the bars, in intellectual circles, in and at the theater, at the races, and at the circus, enticed the Crayon to move among his models unwaveringly and with greatness onto ever-new fields of life. Equipped with a talent which had not yet begun to wane, no longer hindered by formal difficulties, he drew and painted and illustrated in rapid sequence scene after scene, often on the spur of the moment. Various figure studies were later related to contemporary literature, which was much sooner gone and forgotten than Lautrec's illustrations. Often what he scribbled on cardboard was nothing but a spirited allusion, a dedicatory gesture almost undecipherable for later students of his works. The references can only be guessed at, for all his chroniclers have disappeared, and the image returns to what it was at the moment of its inspiration, a picture of life as it presented itself to Lautrec and as he immortalized it beyond his own arduous days.

The sketchy bar scene entitled *Alfred La Guigne* (plate 21) is another representation which we have learned to appreciate for its own values. (Others might be the watercolors brushed as illustrations onto the pages of a novel.) Here the style of the sketch and that of the poster are comparable. It is a sort of repercussion of the solutions regarding surface which were developed in the three-color poster upon a calligraphic style which, while retaining a vibrating nervousness and a sense of the minute, became gradually more sparing in setting. The figure of this man of the world, who occupies a third of

cycling costumes, refers us to the space beyond the picture, to the drinking, talking people with whom the bar is filled. The figure at the right undulates upward like a growing plant and is pure Art Nouveau. Lautrec's goal was the harmony of the contour, so that he found a quick abbreviated sketch quite sufficient for his purposes.

One of the loveliest drawings of its kind demonstrates this beautifully. It depicts the dark-skinned dancer Chocolat (plate 18), partner of the famous English clown, Footit. This superb drawing was executed in India ink and blue pencil.

The scenery is unusually self-sufficient. In a narrow bar, made even narrower by the molelike waiter at the left, a marvelously limber Negro in a tight sporting suit is shown dancing. His cap with its large checks is pulled far down over his bluish face. The chanson, which is still known, is accompanied by a strident lyre plucked by a seated boy with knobby knees. The blackness of the lyre and of a top hat in the background compete with that of Chocolat's raised hand, the most delicate and subtly finished detail of the entire drawing. Here all of Lautrec's fine-nerved abilities can be seen at work. He always knew just when the culminating point in the development of a movement had been reached and his drawings always took into account just how this movement could be credibly realized in the existing space. He achieved this effortlessly, avoiding any possible weakness of form. Everything is fully shaped and, as is usual, the main and secondary figures are finished to differing degrees. There is no longer any possibility of being surprised by the discovery of the disproportionate size of the hand, as in the 1889 drawing of *The Morning After*.

There is a great deal of similarity between what took place in *Chocolat Dancing* and what happens in the study for a *Revue Blanche* poster (plate 19). The sketch represents Missia, wife of Thadée Natanson, one of the directors of the magazine. The best minds of the time—writers, poets, and painters, known and still unknown—came

the scene, is outlined with brownish-purple brush strokes and only his hair, scarf, and bowler hat are hastily colored. The face, barely in profile and briefly indicated in a few telling strokes, remains the color of the ground. On both sides of the figure with its economy of line, the picture comes to life both in color and in drawing. Lautrec goes so far as to reveal his attitude toward this environment. The figure in the broad-brimmed hat leaning her elbow on the bar looks out of the picture with a face which no female clown could possibly surpass. The great feather boa sets off an incomparable moonlike face. To the right, farther back, another female figure, leaning slightly backward and dressed in what looks like one of the first

together in the pages of this review which lasted until 1903. Bonnard, Félix Vallotton, and Lautrec created a new style of illustration here. And Paris received a new kind of homage. Her topography and her citizens have never again been fused together so poetically.

The slight self-consciousness of the drawing, with its multiplicity of short strokes and dots, as well as the way in which the face is half hidden behind a veil and billowing fur, may possibly be explained by Lautrec's encounter with this woman, who was one of the most influential personalities of the time. Known everywhere, she posed here as a graceful skater for the magazine's second poster. The first one had been designed by Bonnard. Once Lautrec painted her more freely, full of charm as she sat in her box at the theater, seen halfway from the back. In the ice-skating scene there is something mute about her as she balances the dark feather fountain on top of her large hat. Her grave face, so very true to life, is conceived almost as a triangle, embedded in the rolls of fur and cut off over the forehead by the straight brim of the hat. One arm dangles rather lifeless and puppetlike in front

of her advancing figure. She keeps her balance with her other arm, which is extended to the right, holding a muff. The sketch tells us only this. In the subsequent poster Lautrec moved the delicate figure of Missia closer toward the observer, as he had done with *Miss May Belfort* at the footlights. Everything has been simplified and given dash. An unforgettable blue-violet, red-dotted dress stands out boldly at the edge of the picture and tapers off at the top to give way to a clearly recognizable gray fur ensemble. The lettering, a carefree stringing together of a varied collection of hand-done letters, is shifted farther to the left and has a place all its own.

In Lautrec's posters the words do not strike us as dead area, for the awkwardness of the lettering stamps them indelibly on our mind, and they are even a continuation of the figural content. Not all Lautrec's thirty-one posters meet this requirement, but only those where he had any say in the formation of the caption characters. Lettering rarely occurred on any of the four hundred lithographs comprised in his work, except in title pages for series, such as the previously mentioned *Yvette Guilbert* and *Elles*, and the consistently exquisite illustrations for Jules Renard's *Histoires naturelles*, as well as title pages for novels, menus, and the like.

The world of the theater comprises a large portion of Lautrec's work. From early youth he had been attracted by costumes and make-up. His studio in Rue Caulaincourt was full to overflowing with Japanese kimonos, masks, and exotic objects of all kinds. He often drew inspiration from the interplay of skin and bright textiles. His models were rarely dressed in everyday, lackluster clothing, but were more likely to be rigged out according to the latest fashions or their profession, with lamps and lights illuminating their features and make-up and intensifying the colors. They were alive to the degree with which they were able to make others forget the simple nature of their being. It would be absurd to imagine them in the court of Lautrec's Château de Malromé or set into a bright summer day in southern France. Three examples from the wealth of pictures, sketches, drawings, and lithographs dealing with the theme of disguise and theater serve to spotlight Lautrec's gift for holding fast the magic of this world in its fantastic transformations. What he transmitted was more than just his own period. He ranks with Watteau and his *Gilles* and with Daumier's visions of the theater. When Lautrec's marvellous female clown, Cha-U-Kao, approaches, Daumier's *Crispin and Scapin* again seem to come to life.

Actually the female clown (plate 20) repeatedly depicted by Lautrec is a being halfway between the dance hall and the theater as she makes her entrance in the Moulin Rouge. Her costume consists of a wide, yellow ruche collar running around a barely perceptible low-cut neckline which boldly frames a delicately painted décolleté, dark green bloomers, and stockings. Cocksure, this unique creature measures all the evening's possibilities with a cool glance as she advances. Yet she never seems to be really working. A great flywheel of revelry is waiting to be set in motion and a mere flip of her finger will set it going madly. Wherever she appeared everything seemed to revolve around her. Larger than life, there is something overwhelmingly clownish in the straddling stance of the figure that reaches all the way up to the white wig and its yellow dangling ribbons. And it endows her with a power of domination from behind this curtain of burlesque mummery. The imperiously flashing eyes betray the faint weariness of a heavy routine. The pained expression so much more common to Lautrec's models than smiles or laughter also draws across her face, with her painted mouth set like a seal on the surrounding powdered surface. The persons who laughed were not the ones Lautrec depicted. He painted with his back to the public; he stayed at the footlights and remained with the actors—the givers and not the takers. The latter served only as walk-ons, as in this superb picture. The clown's companion, wearing a worn cape, as well as the figures in the background, among

whom Lautrec's friend Tristan Bernard is to be seen, emphasize the bemused attitude of Cha-U-Kao who dominates the entire scene.

This also explains the subtle yet dominant diagonal, one of the greatest inventions of the artist, who never seemed to be at a loss for compositional inspirations and had only to pick them out of a flood of images as he produced his paintings or lithographs. Here his pictorial intentions go farther. Color comes into play and the figures grow out of a pale yellow-green ground with the female clown far out in front, cut off at her calves by the edge of the picture. Her companion's huge milky-blue skirt forms a background for the figure up to her hips. Then the dark color that ascends from the base with Cha-U-Kao's legs spreads out, encircling a pink dress at the right and ending only when the sides of the picture have been reached. It continues upward as far as Cha-U-Kao's neck. The upper zone assumes a diffuse color tone similar to that of the floor—the decor of the Moulin Rouge.

Another version of Cha-U-Kao, of which we show a detail (page 49), detracts little from the demonic impression of the painting discussed above. She is standing before us, looking vaguely to the left; her wig and skin complement each other and the ruche collar lies close to her neck. The impression is that of a pastel against a blue ground. Yet the sea-blue eyes, squinting ever so slightly, and the rather sullen set of the pursed lips express a will to dominate the scene through presence alone, to charm an audience and call forth enthusiastic ahs of the kind which resound when the circus master presents a magnificent steed in its solo number.

From the female clown, whose stage is the ballroom, let us proceed to an actual theatrical event: *Marcelle Lender Doing the Bolero in "Chilpéric"* (page 53), an operetta by Hervé, who together with Jacques Offenbach was among the best-loved composers of light opera. Once again we have a celebrity of the times, Marcelle Lender—charming, talented, often painted and drawn by Lautrec. She is better known to the German art public than any

of Lautrec's other figures, for in 1895 a color lithograph *Marcelle Lender en Buste* found its way into the Munich magazine *Pan*, setting off a scandal. Lautrec presented the art historian Julius Meier-Graefe with the whole edition of this famous work, which still occasionally makes its appearance in auctions.

In February, 1895, the operetta was performed by a cast of stars and provided Marcelle Lender with her most successful role as singer and dancer. It was at this time that Lautrec sat more than twenty times at her feet in the Théâtre des Variétés, endlessly sketching, and finally painted a glowing picture of her captivating, orchidlike aspect as she danced. Magic footlights play around her figure, illuminating the pink depths of her long dance dress to amass pale and limpid on her arms and bosom and in her smiling face—quite the opposite effect of natural lighting.

Two antenna-like, giant flowers inserted into her hair repeat the color of the upswirling skirt and transmit a unique charm to the stage space filled with figures. Each face has been touched by the glow of the theater, but it is only a reflection. The figures remain flat, like cardboard props. Not even the dancer at the right, Lender's partner, has any three-dimensional quality or life. And probably he was not intended to, for this leaves all the beauty concentrated on the woman in the light, whose extended foot points toward the footlights, making the figure seem to sway back and forth. This glowing, flesh-and-blood creature is Lautrec's greatest homage to the theater. He concentrated on a single individual, whereas Degas unfurled the great illusion of the world of the theater, filling it with a multiplicity of equally important people.

The magnificence of Marcelle Lender in *Chilpéric* is unsurpassed even by Lautrec's paintings for Armand Sylvestre's and Isidore de Lara's lyric opera *Messalina*, done shortly before his death. These scenes, six in all, of which one of the loveliest, depicting three women seen close up, is reproduced here (page 55), are even more *theater* as well as evidence of Lautrec's late style. They seem to indicate a direction beyond that characteristic of Lautrec, for the colors have become flat and the script of the brush can no longer be deciphered. Magical gray swaths of color move through the picture like ghostly mists, illuminating the statuesque forms as they pass. Only the figure on the right is caught by the footlights and warmed to life on cheek and chin. The background glows deep red. In color it recalls Gauguin; pictorially it seems to anticipate the early works of the Fauves. The subject is no longer a single person, but the whole inebriated state into which one is transferred by the opera.

Turning back once more to the life of the painter, let us glance at a few pictures from his last years, in which he exactly defined his relationship to the figure in space. If desired, many pictures could be aligned which show this in one way or another, but a few are quite sufficient. Lautrec's life was too short to permit him to go beyond the style of his maturity. He had to say what he wanted when he was still young, no older than many of his models, and was required to choose between a cool insight and a heart-warming thirst for beauty. Yet this stage of his life meant more for Lautrec than for a painter who calmly allows his work to mature and learns to bear the fluctuations of his talent with increasing solitude. Lautrec never got that far. He painted until he collapsed both physically and psychically, made a brief comeback, and shortly thereafter died in his mother's arms.

Just once did he manage to develop a real feeling of space: in the picture *Woman at Her Toilet* (page 67), which pertains to the world of the brothels. By looking over the shoulders of the model whose youthful back he showed, he created for himself a point of view which figuratively speaking would have placed the artist on the chandelier. By thus raising himself, as he had with *Yvette Guilbert Taking a Curtain Call* and with the dancing

*La Goulue and Valentin at the Moulin Rouge,* he achieved a naturally receding pictorial space.

The white cloth on which his graceful model sits spreads out freely on all sides. The visible stockinged leg on which the elbow rests gently moves up into the space with an almost imperceptible foreshortening of the thigh. On the floor underneath is a carpet, beyond which the floor boards can be seen, their lines interrupted by woven wicker chairs. The yellow of the wickerwork chairs leads one up higher into the area where the copper-red mass of hair is depicted, that is, behind the model, and then back to the tub standing on the floor. Farther up a blue, softly falling curtain closes off the ascent with an emphasized vertical. The picture as a whole has been simultaneously developed in painting and drawing. There is space in front of the figure, yet she is not lost in it. The slim body is unmistakably that of a particular model; in other words, this is a faithful "portrait" of a specific back. In this sense it is a perfect counterpart to Renoir. The counterbalancing succession of warm skin color and a variety of blue-green tones recalls Degas, although there is something blossomlike in the young body Lautrec depicted and something akin to the heaviness of ripened fruit in the corporeal enchantment of Degas' *Bathers.*

The picture of Justine Dieuhl of 1897 (page 71) is a study of a half nude seated on a divan and turned away from the observer. Still called *Seated Russian Girl* in Joyant's first catalogue, the figure gently makes her way into the space, despite the fact that she is set in a rigid parallel to the picture plane. The painterly quality which hovers over so many of his drawings has become determining here. The short strokes run off in a staccato, yet the picture as a whole remains intact. The mother-of-pearl tones which encompass the skin play around the forms to such an extent that one is reminded of life studies by Bonnard, among which there was probably also one with a black stocking.

Space is expressed differently in two small, sketchlike paintings: *Woman at Her Toilet: Mme. Poupoule* (page 64) and *At the Bar* (page 75). The former, painted in 1898, is in the Toulouse-Lautrec Museum, Albi, and was little known until a few years ago when it captivated the public in a German exhibition with its mysterious charm. In 1951 it was seen by the American public when the Toulouse-Lautrec Museum of Albi sent a collection of Lautrec's work to a traveling exhibition in the United States. The face of this woman at her dressing table, almost hidden under her long, flowing hair, remains almost exactly the tone of the painted wood panel. The features consist of no more than a few highlights on the forehead, tip of the nose, and the chin, while the face, hair, and wall close behind fuse into each other, actually denying spatial depth. The wide, enveloping, blue dressing gown abandons this unison to circumscribe and softly model the bend of the comfortably resting arm and to run into the white coverlet of the dressing table, where picturesque bottles and a cherry-wood box gleam. Only the back side of the mirror propped up at an angle can be seen. The central happening in this pleasant scene is the indolently occupied hands. In their plump delicacy they bring to mind Füssli's London cocotte drawings. Like a second face the fingers of these communicative hands reflect themselves in the mirror. Space here could not possibly be anything but intimate—moving from the cherry-wood box to the knuckles of her hand to the dark under the chin and finally being lost in the hollow between the dressing gown and bosom which is enclosed on either side by her long hair.

This high-grade spatial intimacy, fitted to the inventive drive of the now thirty-four-year-old Lautrec, resulted in a similar *mise en scène* in the Zurich picture *At the Bar* (page 75) of the same year. A couple sit side by side behind the bar, with their glances and thoughts turned in different directions. Monsieur, self-assured, eager for conversation, finds comfort in drink; Madame, calculating and rigid, is turned away and surveys the

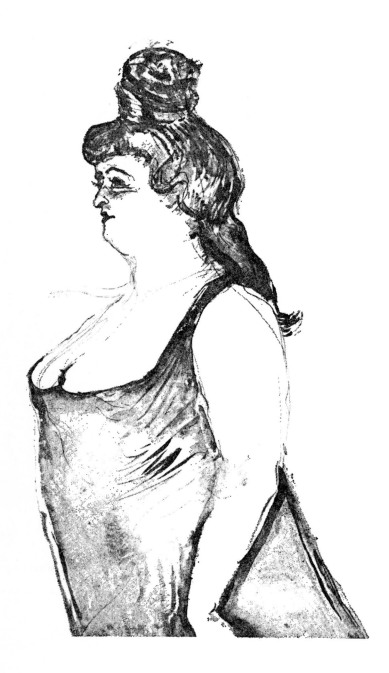

antechamber." This is valid only if the despair read into these figures is valid. It certainly does not coincide with the theories of the antimoralist Lautrec, who verified and observed and as it is would have abandoned and forgotten this bar and this couple long before he could have come to know anything of their moral bankruptcy, or otherwise.

And the space? In the picture of the figure sitting on the floor (page 67) it is self-explanatory; in that of Justine (page 71) it has been stippled in hesitantly and in a riot of color; while with Madame Poupoule (page 64) it loses itself in the warmth of her bosom. In *At the Bar* it is artificially engendered. Here space is won by means of the broad barrier, smooth and shining, which is the bar counter. Behind it the dissimilar hosts appear, filling the mirroring back wall with their contrasting lean and obese forms.

The bottle and glass make the situation sufficiently clear, but even more so does the washed-out appearance of the owner, who peers out between rusty-red patches of hair, whose head seems peculiarly inflated, and whose rust-colored necktie seems to run down his shirt front. But the way in which the back of the man's head with its central part appears in the reflecting plate glass behind him, as isolated as a rising moon, reveals most evidently Lautrec's quiet mockery.

The closing notes of Lautrec's life as a painter are an almost elegiac homage to feminine beauty—not to the venal, attainable, boldly inviting beauty of the girls who followed their animal instincts and in whose proximity he was, but to the unattainable in the person of a lovely passenger on the ship to Spain to whom he offered his platonic homage by immortalizing her, looking out on the ocean, in the poster of an exhibition in the Salon des Cent. The blond, smiling English barmaid (page 77) whom he met in the café concert Star in Le Havre, he drew and painted as he had never done before. This was

hall, assessing profit and loss, as hard as nails. She belongs to Lautrec's clothed class of figures, which were either completely or partially dressed. The half-clothed were for him always on the way to nudity; the fully clothed never. He was no Mannerist. Gotthard Jedlicka said of the couple behind the counter: "Life's jetsam in Death's

The English Barmaid at the Star in Le Havre  1899

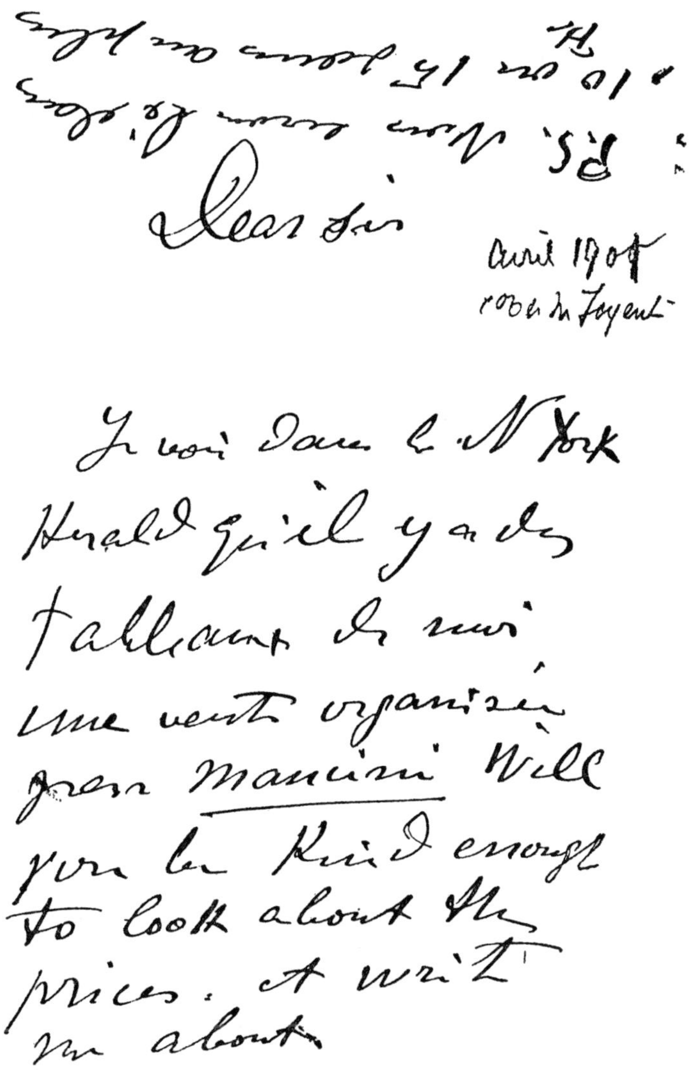

*P.S. ... 10 ou 15 ...*

*Dear Sir*

*avril 1904*
*Château de Joyeux*

*Je vois dans le N York Herald qu'il y a des tableaux de moi une vente organisée pour Mancini. Will you be kind enough to look about the prices. et m'écrit me about*

*J'ai mal aux mollets mais on m'électrise*
*J'ai reçu la bénédiction papale voilà l'âme de Bordeaux*

*il ressemble à lui-même*

*mensongèrement truly yours H*

in 1899. He painted her glowing and happy, her lips parted—not "at work" as with Cha-U-Kao. It is a charming picture, as the related drawing in Albi also is, both of a purity of perception which show that neither wanton women nor the contents of a well-stocked bar could completely destroy Lautrec's sense of beauty. For the first time, with the bright Miss Dolly, he leaves off powder. But if someone should find so much Nature inconsonant with Lautrec, he will still find in this picture the end of the old thread which had unrolled from Albi and Mal-

romé a short generation before to Paris, where the protected child had begun, like other children, to love the pure.

There is also much affection in the picture *The Modiste*, caught in a crepuscular web, of 1900 (page 81). This is Renée Vert, whom he had known for years, and who with friends was to rescue him from his alcoholism. Here she is shown quietly absorbed in her realm of millinery. Lautrec was always free and independent. He painted out of friendship, and the reserve he imposed upon himself here has given this picture the essence of a still life similar to that in Monet's water-lily ponds, which are not as closed in by twilight shadows as the subject is here by feathers and furs. Neither this darkness nor the fact that the features have for the first time become small and delicate can be considered fortuitous.

Lautrec came from the country, and his childhood days were spent among animals. Horses (page 28) and hawks are the noblest of these, as well as dogs. His illustrations for Jules Renard's *Histoires naturelles* and countless other drawings and lithographs, even those meant for amusement, testify to Lautrec's keen vision and his unwavering knowledge as to how animals behave and how they differ. There was a place in his mind for the waddling duck, the turkey, the cock pigeon, and the pug. The ultimate in precision is involved here for the purpose of grasping the specifically typical. Animals do not laugh, and therefore Lautrec did not make them ridiculous, not even Bouboule (plate 23), Madame Palmyre's fat little bulldog. Madame Palmyre was the owner of a restaurant where ladies dressed in the newest male fashions and there Bouboule sat on the counter next to her, an unwitting animal Buddha. With a few quickly fading highlights from the head to the bow legs, Lautrec has enticed her forth from the brown cardboard. This is a masterly drawing, like Lautrec's other animal studies,

whether singly or as part of a scene, as for example that in which Cha-U-Kao enters the Moulin Rouge riding a donkey on Mardi Gras (page 29), when the small gray animals must submit to noise and masquerade.

In a great sweeping movement Lautrec encompassed extremely tranquil subjects and those full of speed and action, to which he dedicated various representations. They included the first bicyclists, the feared first automobilist with a black exhaust cloud streaming out behind, and more familiarly and lovingly the horses and riders with which all his painting began—the race horses and their jockeys, who were no bigger than he himself was. Here Lautrec was often a resurrected Géricault. The preparatory drawing and the subsequent lithograph *The Jockey* of 1899 (plate 24) probably are most closely connected with the instantaneous photography which was then coming to the fore. This work, unique among all earlier and later horse pictures, was to have begun a series of racing scenes—*Courses*—which was never realized.

With the extreme exertion of a racing horse, we are led out of the world of the Moulin Rouge, away from the diseased and wild nights of Montmartre into full daylight, into the fresh air of the race course where windmills can be seen on the horizon, where a clean wind blows and the legend of the perversity of the painter Henri de Toulouse-Lautrec Monfa is definitely dispersed.

# Chronology

1864 On November 24, Henri-Marie-Raymond de Toulouse-Lautrec Monfa was born in his parents' château in Albi, the son of Count Alphonse de Toulouse-Lautrec and his cousin, the Viscountess Adèle, born Tapié de Céleyran. His youth was spent in the Château du Bosc, Albi, and Céleyran, and later in Paris, where he went to school. His talent for drawing was already evident when he was a child.

1878 He slipped in the Château du Bosc and broke a leg. The following year he broke his other leg while visiting in Barèges. This second accident crippled him and his legs remained stunted.

1881 After receiving his degree in Toulouse he went to Paris, where he began his painting studies under René Princeteau, a deaf-mute animal painter and friend of his father.

1882 Transferal to the atelier of the Academy professor Léon Bonnat and from there to the atelier of Fernand Cormon. Collaboration with Émile Bernard. Encounter with Van Gogh.

1885 He rented a studio in Rue Caulaincourt, where he lived about thirteen years. He generally worked in Montmartre, particularly in dance halls, cabarets, and in the circus.

1889–90 Exhibited in the Salon des Indépendants and with the group "Les XX" in Brussels.

1891 The first poster.

1892 First color lithographs, especially of Yvette Guilbert and Jane Avril. Until 1895 he worked increasingly in the brothels.

1893 The Goupil Gallery exhibited his work for the first time on the Boulevard Montparnasse.

1894 Trip to Brussels.

1895 Active in the printers' workshops. He painted two curtains for La Goulue's show booth after she had been forced to leave the Moulin Rouge. Repeated trips to London. Journeys to Spain and Holland.

1898 His health deteriorated.

1899–1900 A breakdown necessitated his recovery for several months in a sanatorium in Neuilly, near Paris, where he drew from memory a series of drawings dedicated to the circus. When his health improved he returned to his Paris studio, traveled to Bordeaux, Le Havre, Arcachon, and visited his mother in the Château de Malromé.

1901 Another breakdown. He traveled to his mother at Malromé and died there September 9.

1  Guenle de Bois (The Morning After)  1889

2  Seated Dancer  1890

3  The Laundress  1888

4  Dr. Péan Operating  1891

5 At the Foot of the Scaffold 1893

6  La Goulue and Valentin at the Moulin Rouge  1891

7   The Englishman at the Moulin Rouge   1892

8  Aristide Bruant  1893
   Study for the lithograph

9  Aristide Bruant  1893  ▷
   Lithograph

10   Cover for L'Estampe Originale   1893

11  Jane Avril  1893

12  Yvette Guilbert's Gloves  1894

13   Yvette Guilbert Taking a Curtain Call   1894

14  Woman in Bed  1894

15. The Cabaret Entertainer
Caudieux 1893

16  Monsieur, Madame, and Dog (The Proprietors of a Brothel)  1893

17 The Two Friends
1894

18  Chocolat Dancing  1896

19  Missia Natanson  1895

20   At the Moulin Rouge. The Clowness Cha-U-Kao   1895

21  Alfred La Guigne  1894

22  Mademoiselle Lucie Bellanger  1896

# List of Colorplates

Page 9    *Portrait of Vincent van Gogh.* 1887. Pastel on cardboard, $22^1/_2 \times 18^1/_2''$. Stedelijk Museum, Amsterdam

Page 15   *Portrait of Mr. Warrener.* 1892. Tempera on cardboard, $22^7/_8 \times 18^7/_8''$. Toulouse-Lautrec Museum, Albi. Study for the color lithograph *The Englishman at the Moulin Rouge*

Page 21   *Jane Avril at the Jardin de Paris.* 1893. Color lithographic poster, $51^1/_8 \times 37^3/_8''$

Page 25   *Jane Avril Leaving the Moulin Rouge.* 1892. Gouache on cardboard, $33^1/_4 \times 25''$. Wadsworth Atheneum, Hartford, Connecticut. Bequest of George A. Gay, 1941

Page 33   *The Salon in the Rue des Moulins.* 1894. Oil on canvas, $43^1/_4 \times 51^1/_8''$. Toulouse-Lautrec Museum, Albi

Page 35   *The Tattooed Woman.* 1894. Tempera on cardboard, $24^1/_2 \times 18^7/_8''$. Collection Hans R. Hahnloser, Bern. Scene from a brothel

Page 39   *Marcelle.* 1894. Tempera on cardboard, $18^1/_8 \times 11^1/_2''$. Toulouse-Lautrec Museum, Albi

Page 43   *Girl Putting On Her Stockings.* 1894. Oil and gouache on cardboard, $23^5/_8 \times 16^7/_8''$. Toulouse-Lautrec Museum, Albi

Page 47   *Portrait of Gabriel Tapié de Céleyran.* 1894. Oil on canvas, $43^1/_4 \times 22''$. Toulouse-Lautrec Museum, Albi

Page 49   *The Clowness Cha-U-Kao* (detail). 1895. Oil tempera on cardboard, full size $31^7/_8 \times 23^5/_8''$. Collection Mrs. Frank J. Gould, New York

Page 53   *Marcelle Lender Doing the Bolero in "Chilpéric."* 1895. Oil on canvas, $57^1/_2 \times 57^7/_8''$. Collection The Hon. and Mrs. John Hay Whitney, New York

Page 55   *"Messalina."* 1900. Oil on canvas, $36^1/_2 \times 26^3/_4''$. Collection E. G. Bührle, Zurich

Page 67   *Woman at Her Toilet.* 1896. Oil on cardboard, $25^5/_8 \times 20^7/_8''$. The Louvre, Paris

Page 71   *Justine Dieuhl.* 1897. Tempera on cardboard, $23 \times 18^7/_8''$. Private collection

Page 75   *At the Bar.* 1898. Oil tempera on cardboard, $32 \times 23^5/_8''$. Kunsthaus Zurich

Page 77   *The English Barmaid at the Star in Le Havre.* 1899. Tempera on panel, $16^1/_8 \times 12^7/_8''$. Toulouse-Lautrec Museum, Albi

Page 81   *The Modiste.* 1900. Oil tempera on panel, $24 \times 19^3/_8''$. Toulouse-Lautrec Museum, Albi

*Photographic credits:* Toulouse-Lautrec Museum, Albi; Schmolz-Huth, Cologne; The Toledo Museum of Art, Ohio; Georges Groc, Toulouse; Sterling and Francine Clark Art Institute, Williamstown, Massachusetts; Dr. Oskar Reinhart, Winterthur, Switzerland

# List of Black-and-White Plates

1 *Guenle de Bois (The Morning After)*. 1889. India ink and blue pencil, $18^7/_8 \times 24^3/_4''$. Toulouse-Lautrec Museum, Albi

2 *Seated Dancer*. 1890. Charcoal heightened with white, $19^5/_8 \times 15^3/_4''$. Collection Saincère, Paris

3 *The Laundress*. 1888. Lithographic crayon, $26^3/_4 \times 22^3/_4''$

4 *Dr. Péan Operating*. 1891. Gouache on cardboard, $29 \times 19^1/_2''$. Sterling and Francine Clark Art Institute, Williamstown, Massachusetts

5 *At the Foot of the Scaffold*. 1893. Tempera, oil, watercolor, and charcoal on paper, $28^3/_4 \times 22^7/_8''$. Private collection, Cologne. Study for the poster

6 *La Goulue and Valentin at the Moulin Rouge*. 1891. Charcoal and gouache, $60^5/_8 \times 46^1/_2''$. Toulouse-Lautrec Museum, Albi. Preparatory drawing for the poster

7 *The Englishman at the Moulin Rouge*. 1892. Color lithograph, $18^1/_2 \times 14^5/_8''$

8 *Aristide Bruant*. 1893. Charcoal drawing, $12^1/_2 \times 8^1/_2''$. Private collection, Frankfort. Study for the lithograph

9 *Aristide Bruant*. 1893. Lithograph, $10^1/_4 \times 8^1/_4''$

10 *Cover for L'Estampe originale*. 1893. Lithograph, $22 \times 25^1/_4''$. Magazine cover, prior to the addition of color and lettering

11 *Jane Avril*. 1893. Oil tempera on cardboard, $31^1/_8 \times 19^5/_8''$. Study for *L'Estampe originale*

12 *Yvette Guilbert's Gloves*. 1894. Tempera on cardboard, $24^5/_8 \times 14^3/_4''$. Toulouse-Lautrec Museum, Albi

13 *Yvette Guilbert Taking a Curtain Call*. 1894. Gouache, $18^7/_8 \times 9^7/_8''$. Toulouse-Lautrec Museum, Albi

14 *Woman in Bed*. 1894. Tempera on cardboard, $18^1/_2 \times 18^1/_8''$. Toulouse-Lautrec Museum, Albi

15 *The Cabaret Entertainer Caudieux*. 1893. Tempera on paper, $30^1/_4 \times 20^7/_8''$. Toulouse-Lautrec Museum, Albi

16 *Monsieur, Madame, and Dog. (The Proprietors of a Brothel)*. 1893. Oil tempera on canvas, $18^7/_8 \times 23^5/_8''$. Toulouse-Lautrec Museum, Albi

17 *The Two Friends*. 1894. Tempera on cardboard, $18^1/_2 \times 13''$. Toulouse-Lautrec Museum, Albi

18 *Chocolat Dancing*. 1896. India ink and blue pencil, heightened with white, $30^1/_4 \times 24''$. Toulouse-Lautrec Museum, Albi

19 *Missia Natanson*. 1895. Colored charcoal drawing on paper, $58^1/_4 \times 41^3/_8''$. Toulouse-Lautrec Museum, Albi. Study for the poster for the *Revue Blanche*

20 *At the Moulin Rouge. The Clowness Cha-U-Kao*. 1895. Oil on canvas, $29^1/_2 \times 21^5/_8''$. Collection Dr. Oskar Reinhart, Winterthur, Switzerland

21 *Alfred La Guigne*. 1894. Gouache on cardboard, $25^3/_4 \times 19^3/_4''$. National Gallery of Art, Washington, D.C. Chester Dale Collection

22 *Mademoiselle Lucie Bellanger*. 1896. Tempera on cardboard, $31^1/_8 \times 23^5/_8''$. Toulouse-Lautrec Museum, Albi

23 *Bouboule, the bulldog of Madame Palmyre*. 1897. Tempera on cardboard, $22 \times 16^1/_2''$. Toulouse-Lautrec Museum, Albi

24 *The Jockey*. 1899. Color lithograph, $20^1/_4 \times 14^1/_8''$

# List of Text Illustrations

Page 6   *The Quadrille of Musical Chairs.* 1886. Chalk, $17^3/_4 \times 22^1/_2''$. Toulouse-Lautrec Museum, Albi. Preparatory sketch

Page 11   *The Clowness Cha-U-Kao at the Nouveau Cirque.* Chalk

Page 13   *In the Wings at the Folies-Bergère.* 1896. India ink and blue pencil, $30^1/_4 \times 24''$. Toulouse-Lautrec Museum, Albi

Page 19   Page of a letter in which Lautrec discusses the French fabulist La Fontaine

Page 23   *Miss May Belfort at the Irish and American Bar.* 1895. Lithograph, $12^5/_8 \times 10^1/_4''$

Page 27   *The Laundress.* 1888. Charcoal drawing on Ingres paper, $23^5/_8 \times 15^3/_4''$. Toulouse-Lautrec Museum, Albi

Page 28   *Cantering Horse.* Pen and ink, $9^1/_2 \times 6^1/_4''$. The Art Institute of Chicago. From a sketchbook

Page 29   *La Redoute: Cha-U-Kao's Entrance at the Moulir on Mardi Gras.* 1896. India ink, heightened v    ,  $38^1/_8 \times 28^3/_4''$. Toulouse-Lautrec Museum

Page 30   *La Goulue and Valentin.* 1894. Lit⁾      $11^3/_4 \times 9''$

Page 32   *Caricature: The Judgement of*       en and ink

Page 37   *Caricature: Gabriel Ta⁷*      *⸴eyran.* 1894. Pen and ink, $13 \times 8^5/_8''$. Toulouse-    ᵣec Museum, Albi

Page 41   *Yvette Guilbert.* 1894. Charcoal drawing on paper, heightened with color, $73^1/_4 \times 36^5/_8''$. Toulouse-Lautrec Museum, Albi

Page 46   *The Dramatist Romain Coolus* (detail of ꙮ the Théâtre de l'Œuvre). Lithograph

Page 59   *Woman from a Brothel.* Red chal⁾

Page 61   *Jane Avril Dancing.* 1893. ⸱            on cardboard, $38^5/_8 \times 27^5/_8''$. Collection ⁷          ⸴is. Study for the poster

Page 62   Above, left: *Hen·            ᴊe-Lautrec, Self-Caricature* (detail of a m⸴          Lithograph
Above, rig⁾          ᴌue. Red chalk
Below, ⁾          ᴊuilbert. 1893. Drawing, $9^7/_8 \times 7^1/_2''$
Belo⸴          ᴊrcelle Lender, the Actress. Chalk drawin⸴

Page 6            ᴊx *Dancing at the Petit-Casino.* 1893. Litho-ᵣh, $10^5/_8 \times 8^1/_4''$

*Woman at Her Toilet: Mme. Poupoule.* 1898. Oil tempera on panel, $24 \times 16''$. Toulouse-Lautrec Museum, Albi

Page 66   *Head of a Woman, Right Profile.* Lead pencil, $5 \times 3^7/_8''$. Toulouse-Lautrec Museum, Albi

Page 69   *"Reine de Joie"* (detail). 1892. Lithographic crayon. Study for the poster advertising Victor Joze's novel

Page 76   *Mademoiselle Cocyte in "La Belle Hélène," Bordeaux.* 1900. Drawing, $14^3/_4 \times 11^3/_8''$. Toulouse-Lautrec Museum, Albi. Study for the watercolor

Page 79   Letter from Lautrec to his friend Maurice Joyant. April, 1901

Page 80   Animal studies for the illustrations for Jules Renard's *Histoires naturelles*